THE AGENCY OF BLISS

THE AGENCY OF BLISS

emilee baum trucks

ANT BEAR PRESS

First Edition, January 2012.

Copyright © 2012 by Emilee Baum Trucks.
All rights reserved.

Trucks, Emilee Baum
The Agency of Bliss / Emilee Baum Trucks

ISBN 978-0-615-44845-9

Epigram from Śāntideva, *The Bodhicaryavatara: A Guide to the Buddhist Path of Awakening*. Translated by Kate Crosby and Andrew Skilton. Birmingham: Windhorse Publications, 2002. Print.

Published in the United States of America by Emilee Baum Trucks with Ant Bear Press.

Manufactured in the United States of America.

*for the mothers
and the other mothers*

CONTENTS

my story for you

APPLE

5   refuge
7   frames
9   apple pomegranate lotus
15 woods
19 gingerbread
21 the bed in which I am conceived one
25 dire wolf
27 cannot afford these artifacts
29 the dalai lama says sprout
31 plunge
33 line drawing
35 rabbit
37 floorboards
39 victorian violins
41 apologist
43 ways unfed
45 treegarden
49 peripheral vision

POMEGRANATE

53 yellow submarine
55 red door in the south
59 meat grinder
61 photograph
65 stone setting

67	modeling one
71	general store
73	on the bus
75	beach lady
77	modeling two
83	warrior stance
85	stars
87	cowgirl
91	you teach then
93	the queen's path

LOTUS

97	formulae
99	chamber music
101	rehearsal
103	sun salutation
107	white dog
111	dakinis
113	tuesday
115	wind up
117	the other mother
123	demoness
125	artmaking
127	the bed in which I am conceived two
129	dedicating the merits

source material

endnotes

afterward

After first assessing the full implications, one should either begin or not begin. Surely, not beginning is better than turning back once one has begun.

Come here.

Here, right here

right next to me, now.

Sit down.

Stop. Now:

Listen.

Listen to me.

Let me tell you.

Listen.

This is my story for you.

And then,

I go for refuge.

I've taken refuge many times, even officially once. Today, I go for refuge. I am not taking it passively from another. Today I actively go for refuge, seek it out with every bit of my being.

I go for refuge to the embodiment of the awakened mind. Every person has the capacity for awakening, including myself. To my teachers, I go for refuge.

I go for refuge to the wisdom of the path, to the knowledge that has been hidden and revealed in this world. I go for refuge to the community of like-minded beings, no matter where I meet them or how they appear. I am not alone on this journey, though I am the only one that can walk my path.

I go for refuge in these things, I continually aspire to the sweet refuge of these life-giving things, because I seek to embody awakening mind. I will continue to seek refuge in these things so that my journey will be ever quickening, and so that I may ever more effectively enable the awakening of all beings everywhere.

And then,

I set up a frame.

There are lots of awkward thresholds knocking about, angles, knees and elbows jutting. Frames of varying sizes bumping into each other, cramped headspace. Not these doors, we are not climbing through these, not yet. I remember being there before, I know I will have to go there again, but not right now.

No, keep going. Steady, slowly. Confident, passing familiar thresholds, branching hallways. Sometimes there are other beings in these rooms, up and down stairwells. Go on, we're not here to see them.

Breathe deep, new doorways. There's a doorway that I'm here to see. Echoes become louder. Less familiar, less friendly. Unexplored turns, menacing corridors. It is okay, I think, you have a reason to be here. No one will stop you.

A turn, a turn, a turn again. And then,

There is a doorway. It is a black doorway, lacquered. It is a heavy door, with a large knob. A single word is inscribed on the door, and it says

(*kallisti*)

Something you can't make out. The writing is calligraphic, somehow spidery. Hand on knob, gingerly at first, and then with increasing confidence.

Feeling the weight and smoothed softness, the history of lifetimes of touches, caressing the knob, it is heavy. It alternates cold and warm in my palm.

Turning easily, silently, to the left, the knob gives rise to tumblers falling into place. The door swings open

And then,

I am barefoot in a courtyard. Buildings on all sides, brick and weathered wood, boarding school, institution. Breathing into my body, focusing on feeling the dream, the shape of me here. The grass between my toes, the air on my skin. I walk to the wall, move between buildings, brick under fingers. Mossy.

A hand-lettered sign with an arrow hangs on the wall. Peering, it seems to say student academic services. I should go there, I think, I am a student after all, and so I walk in the direction it points. Coming to a narrow place between two taller buildings, a thin storm drain runs a channel of water in the center of the path. Moving between, running hands across brick, something slimy not moss under my fingertips. My heartbeat quickens and I decide to not think about it too hard, just keep moving forward. Voices bounce ahead, and I do not want to meet them in this darker, narrow channel.

Coming out from between the buildings, two groundskeepers look up. One, standing closer to me, holds a long garden hose in his hands, watering the trees. He lurches toward me, gap-toothed, bib-all, unkempt. He swings his hose and says, Do you know how to get the fingers in the holes, under the girls' titties? He is grinning.

The first fingers of fear jab me in the stomach. There is slight danger here, possibility of distraction. This dream is not about them. Excuse me? I say, politely smiling.

He lurches closer, fingers grasping and bulbous, a little bit of spittle. He is somehow disproportionate, but I can't get a fix on how. The girls, the girls' titties, how do you get your fingers in the holes, in the holes of the girlies? How do you do it, the holes under the titties?

With clarity, I think to myself: If I just ask him where student academic services are, he will have to complete the formula and tell me where to go. He will respond according to script and I can walk away.

Can you tell me where the student academic services are? I ask, and he replies as if by rote memory, telling me to go back there and take the door to the left, go up the stairs, look for room two-oh-eight or two-eighteen.

Thank you, I say, and turn to walk away.

So, how do you get the fingers into the holes of the girls? he calls, water from his limp garden hose running uselessly onto cobblestones, down the drain.

Maybe you should ask the girls, I reply, walking away.

I walk back to the door leading into the stairwell. Moving, I become aware of being followed by a little boy, maybe ten or twelve years old. He is overweight, wearing shorts and a t-shirt that are too tight for him, his belly peeking. He is filthy, covered with dirt and mud, trailing me at a distance.

I speed up a little, pull open the door to the stairwell. Sunlight slants through the windows and it has a strong, musty smell, like the basement of a library warm with old heaters in the winter. It is a familiar smell and I smile, a smell associated with knowledge, institutions of learning. I take one step up, two.

I turn and look back out the window in the door, and see the little boy approaching. Becoming nervous again. Looking up the stairwell it is suddenly far too narrow and steep, there is no way I can squeeze my body through. I start to push, I know the trick, but my panic continues to rise and constrict, I have to get up these stairs, he will be in here any moment, those impossibly small stairs. What does he want? Why is he following me?

The door flies open, but the little boy isn't standing there. Instead, I am standing there, myself at maybe three or five years old. I back down the two steps I'd managed to climb, unsure. This is not the first time I've met myself in dreams, this young self. I've learned to listen to what she has to say.

She takes my hands. Her words are whispered, interconnected, impressions. She presses into my right palm three round objects: a dime, flattened like in those stretch-a-penny machines found in tourist traps. A coin from a realm I do not recognize. A medallion with a star and spirals on the face.

Use what's left of the curse, she says. There is something urgent in her speech, a sense of perplexity at why I am wasting my time trying to climb these stairs. What are you doing here? she asks, How will you use this? She curls the fingers of my right hand around the three tokens, closing them into my fist. Then, she takes up my left hand.

Look for the red, for the apples. The apples, what's left of the apples, the red, what are you doing here, she whispers. I see the boy looking on through the window. She pushes a ring into my left hand, and I slip it onto my fingers, the index or the third, I can't quite tell. An oval stone with three pips on either side. And then she is gone, out the door, disappeared.

Looking up again at the stairs, feeling the certainty of what she said, sure of the soundness of her words. Why am I wasting my time in this particular tower? Going back into the courtyard I scan the pale and mossy grounds, looking for any sign of red. All colors fade and I see it then: an apple.

I pick it up and examine it closely: red and black and gold, bruised in some places where it rolled on the ground. Her words were echoing in my head, already becoming unformed, and looking at the apple my senses accelerate, the vividness of awakening even more in the dream. Peering at the apple, poring over it, deciding with a most urgent and ravenous mouth: I will eat it, I will eat the reddest part of the apple I can find, I will consume it, put it in my body.

Finding the spot and biting it deeply, surprise. Not too sweet, not too crisp, not of any apple tasted before. White and soft and not soft, the apple in my hand. Seeking any sign of red. Apples are scattered on the ground sparsely here, gone unnoticed before, leading to an archway.

Walking, my tokens in my right hand and bitten apple in my left, I leave the courtyard. The hill rises into an orchard, where this apple originates. I look up at the trees, reach up, jump, will myself into the boughs to get a fresher apple. Doing so I notice these are not apples at all, or not just apples. Examining them more closely, I sink slowly back to earth, feet planting in the grass of the orchard.

At the base, these swollen apples have a stem that look like the crown of pomegranates, a deep red color. Those mouths of skin and flesh fold backward in blooming to reveal seeds like pomegranates or figs, a deep red color. Dropping seeds, the fruit then opens further to the fullness of a lotus flower, white and red petals arching to ripeness before dropping off the tree. As I watch, the orchard is blooming and dying and regenerating before me, stretching out across the hills, time accelerating.

Overhead, a thunderous sky menaces, deep clouds of thunderstorms rolling toward the orchard. A warm strange wind lifts my hair, and the color drains from the world. The scene becomes shades of gray, save the urgent red of the apples. Time is growing short.

Looking at the coins in my hand, studying them, trying to remember. Feeling there is not much time, I don't have long, focusing concentration to read the inscription there, to memorize what is seen.

The effort breaks the dream

And then,

I am in the woods. These are the woods of my childhood, my territory. It is where I first roamed freely. I know every inch of these woods, am surefooted over every terrain in this circumscribed area. I know the boundaries, the in-between places between my woods and the other woods. I have even named some of the places in my woods, gathering places, meeting places used to give direction.

These woods know me. They have watched me build forts and mimic household life, they witnessed and provided supplies for my neighborhood wars. They saw me walk the length of the stream barefoot, from the tunnels to the ivy. In these woods, I wrote my first poem in a meadow. In these woods, I smoked my first stolen cigarette.

I was in a different place then. I know you know what I'm talking about. It was a different way of seeing the world. Younger, with a different kind of wisdom. I always knew where to walk, paying attention to my feet, because I always had my nose in a book. I knew my place in the world because I could hear it all around me, could feel it pulsing in my peripheral vision. My feet knew which trails to take, pavement or pounded dirt, ditches or drain pipes. This is your back yard, and you know every leaf that grows on every bush, head of the summer in the thick of the woods. Sometimes the cicadas would buzz so loud you couldn't hear anyone speak and so you just had to wait.

I am standing at the stream in my back yard, the result of runoff from a huge storm drain in a ravine next to my house. There are ways that I know things that I don't really remember now how I knew. Half-remembered dreams, figments of imagination. I tried on all kinds of ways of knowing, practicing believing impossible things. As many as ten in one morning, says the queen.

One way I practice believing impossible things is by story telling. Never mind that I don't usually tell stories, you have to start somewhere. My road as a writer-child appears fraught with danger, and humor helps keep the creepiness at bay. Sometimes even the most beautiful sunlit day can be carved out by the cool underwater of possibility. Every choice is one of intention.

No longer running from my own legs. That is, I appear to be running, might as well do so, might as well tell the story. When you find yourself running, you must determine where you would like to go, because chances are you'll get there in a hurry. To know where you're going, have a look at where you are.

This can be a real challenge sometimes, especially when you're running like hell. Like waking up and realizing you're just a super-under-cover regular person. You're so ordinary and unimportant you just slide all over the place without breaking the surface tension.

I am watching water spiders try and cross over the deep place by the old tree. The water near the curved bank is shallow and clear, but it takes a long time to navigate the whole periphery. If you go across the middle, the distance is shorter, but much deeper. Much deeper, and it stays still most of the time. Except for when things from below come up and eat whatever tries to cross there.

I feel this way as a writer as a child, above and below and behind and all over the damn place. Endless doorways of attention. Waking up with words on your tongue, songs in your chest.

Telling the dream of the magician cutting your tongue out, or the dream of going from hut to hut, house to house, both welcomed and ashamed.

Or the dream of the purple dinner plate breaking, the plate for the most beautiful thing. She died. Everyone wept in that dream.

And then,

I am wandering through other woods too, different than mine. Darker woods, where bitter apples grow on leafless trees. The woods that are on the way to grandma's house, the one with breadcrumb trails. See how the branches grow together here, tighter, more closely knit? Vines weave and dense leaves cover the light. The sound changes, and I become aware of rustlings and chirpings, the path becomes less roaming and more prescribed. Guided, intended. The woods crowd in closer, rubbernecking, trying to get a good look at the young thing wandering here.

I am walking slower. I am listening much more carefully. My nostrils flare and I take a deep breath. I come into a clearing

And then,

I am sleeping in the bed in which I was conceived. Dreaming, grandmother's house, sitting room parlor, sipping. There's no flying in the house. Miniature toy dogs, miniature houses, articulated limbs. Light diffused by curtains.

Faded blue bows and yellowed lace. Roses once red gone pink. Thick glass artifacts on dustless shelves, rows of perfume bottles and salt and pepper shakes. The one chair in the corner, next to the book shelf, near the foot of the stairs in the mostly-finished basement. Nap of dark carpet over concrete, the padding of my feet fleeing imagined threats up the stairs. My grandmother's basement, where she keeps her sewing machine and AVON perfume bottles and porcelain sculptures of bald eagles.

My grandmother's basement, it is a cave. We are in the bedroom behind the long room, the one that takes so long to cross, full of so many things precariously balanced. The bedroom with the red carpet and the porcelain tiger statues chained together with delicate silver loops.

Students are seated in a circle around a low fire. We are talking, and chanting, discussing, and all have our notebooks with us. I am hearing myself talking, I am writing, I am hearing voices chanting and singing, the drum, the lopsided walking of five legs.

And then there is a breath of silence, and people are closing their books and preparing to leave. I am holding a pen and a book in my hands. The writing is scrawled in a continuous scribe across the page: yesyesyesyesyesyesyes

My teacher kisses my cheek and reassures me with her love woman voice. I feel slow, confused, a little bit stupid. It is four or five in the morning, dawn will arise soon, people have to wake early to leave the next day. I feel guilty, somehow responsible. We are returning to our rooms, disperse in all directions. Some out the back door, some into the pantry, some up the stairs, some under the couches. They are slithering out in all kinds of ways, adding to my disquiet.

We cross the big room, and I am remembering how I used to sing myself across this space, alone as a little girl. I was terrified then, of what I couldn't say, making that crossing alone. If there were such thing as monsters, they live near here.

I sing my little song to myself, trying to piece together what happened as we walk up the stairs. I can see the sidelong looks now, hear the whispering and scuttling. Faces of other students passing into shadow, eyes wide, mouths covered.

Let me see it, a student says, as we emerge from the stairwell and into the kitchen. You may not think it's much, but you're a master. I become very anxious, clutch my book to my chest. He stops me at the kitchen table, a circle of solitary light. There are groups of girls in the darkness watching, whispering.

I thought I had just been writing and talking. Realizing I don't know what is in my book, a cold finger of fear worms in me. Don't remember what just happened, whatever it was, and it was big. I had sat in a circle all through the night in my mother's mother's basement and I didn't remember what was written here, what I'd shown.

I struggle with my desire to run to the bedroom I share with my sister and shut the door, to look at what is in my book alone. Instead, I sit down at the table with him, opening. The others nearby hover closer. I feel so thick, trying to remember, trying to retrace my steps, looking at the pages and trying to remember what comes next.

This page here, writing. I remember this, early on in the evening. Pages turn and the writing becomes unstructured, loops and leaps across the page. I remember this, not this specifically, but this kind of writing happens in other journals. Some of it is legible, some I have to intuit.

I turn again and suddenly color leaps across the page, feeling a sinking in my stomach. There is a picture of water with an approach or feeling of descending. The lines are initially sloppy, color not filled in, but the drawings become increasingly precise as the pages turn.

Then, there is a feeling of being deeper. A picture of her koi, drawn as leviathan.

There are grottoes. The light lessens, disappears. And then, a shifting veil of water, I turn the page and suddenly outlines of drawings of children, Dick and Jane, appear in bright red. The interiors of the figures are starkest white, but the children are defined in bright red. I would recognize their cherubic bodies anywhere. Here they are playing; here they are going to school. Her curls frame her face perfectly, and I can imagine them all colored in. But drawn here in my book they are white, with red outlines, and outside the red is that shifting blue veil of ocean.

How did I do that, I think to myself, and lean in for a closer look. In the shifting ocean I see by the pen stroke that the red lines were drawn first, defining form and emptiness. The background is completely filled in with the shifting ocean, covering a two page spread. Dozens of pairs of precisely drawn dicks and janes, from sea to shining sea.

On the next page, a man's face emerges from the water, blue pencil giving way to gray graphite. At first, I don't recognize him at all, no recollection of making this drawing, and coldness grips my chest. Then, seeing he has been drawn in profile, a quarter turn to the right, I remember laughing around the fire talking about him. He looks like Willie Nelson, and that makes me laugh, oddly comforted. I am intrigued. My giddiness grows, knowing the next page will be a complete surprise.

It is a rabbit. It is also a mask. It is also somehow a tracing of my hand. It is colored simply, but in the figure very precise shapes have been cut out for eye holes. You can turn the page and hold it up to your face and it is a mask. Showing this page, I feel self-conscious hesitation, the agitation of the others who are watching. Sensing the change in feeling, I take up my book and make to leave, but not before holding up the page and looking at them all through my mask. Breathing hard, heart pounding, wake up wet with sweat

And then,

I am driving through cool hollers in northeast Tennessee. The shadows and long sun roll deep between the trees, and the wind is turning chill with the changing leaves. Winding through the hills, my windows are down, wind and cigarette smoke. I am listening to mountain music *when I awoke / a dire wolf / six hundred pounds of sin /was grinning / at my window / all I said was / come on in*

Don't murder me, I sing along. I am going to see an old friend, someone I haven't known very long. I think about the dire wolf, and imagine myself sitting in that cabin. A plain room way away in the mountains, shifting patterns of light and time. A dusty bottle, clean liquor, grenadine. It is raining outside, lightening flashes, and that face is grinning at my window. Come on in, I say, and keep singing to myself *the wolf came in / I got my cards/ we sat down for a game / I cut my deck to the queen of spades / but the cards were all the same*

Sitting across the table from me, all tongue and teeth and eyeballs. My, grandma, what large eyes you have, I think. The better to see me with, hungry eyes. Devouring eyes, eating me up, ripe for the plucking. What fine fur you have, what a fine smile. What a grinning, lolling tongue you have. Look at this basket of goodies I've brought you. Teeth.

Then I am Little Red, and I am thinking about my mother. She grew up in this part of the world, her family has roots here. I was born in the west and educated in the northeast, but much of my raising comes from the south. Her nickname is Red, my father has called her that as long as memory.

He also calls her Toad. In their young and saucier days, mom had a little golf polo with a frog embroidered on the chest, and he liked to point it out and make her blush.

Here I am, little red, riding the hood. Little red, subtle red, left hand, southern door. The game begins, and the wolf salivates on my thigh. I cut the deck of cards

And then,

I am staying in a huge manor house filled with many guests. There is an event happening, but a mystery as well, a game like Agatha Christie's *Ten Little Indians*. The guests are all very well dressed and walking through the gardens, seeing and being seen. They are erecting a pavilion there for a wedding. People are arriving for the celebration, and many porters hustle back and forth, lugging carts of leather, traveling trunks stamped with exotic locales. Next to the brass and shiny buttons of the porters' uniforms, these world beaten trunks thump of authority and safaris and old money.

I grow bored of being underfoot, dodging all the hustle and bustle, and wander. The house and grounds are filled with all kinds of odd artifacts and curiosities. In the garden and around the reflecting pool are perverse and beautiful sculptures, terrible likenesses and abstract emotions. Inside the manor, the rooms and hallways twist and turn disproportionately, long sparse halls and spiral staircases and windows in odd places. Every room is filled with knickknacks and immense furniture of history: Americana bottle caps and gentleman's dart boards from the 1700s and potsherds and tiny stone great mother sculptures and giant replicas of Andy Warhol's Chairman Mao paintings.

Everything, absolutely everything has a tiny white price tag, attached with some light cotton string.

I wander up and down the hallways, through the galleries, seek out odd doors. In every room, I look at items that catch my eye; I look at the price tag. I try and figure out the person who has priced these things, valued them in such bold, black script.

A family-heritage King James Bible. A Tibetan thangka. An old lithograph in a beautiful but battered frame of a strong jawed woman with smooth dark hair, holding a grinning baby. Books, piles and piles of books. Preserved circus posters. Music boxes, old dusty mirrors the size of entire walls in huge gold frames. Priceless pieces and dime store junk, I look at all of their prices.

Then somehow I am there with her, the woman who owns all this. She is the intended bride, determined to have her wedding. There is another woman, a mistress, and they are fighting for a man who is oblivious to their war. Somehow they know I know, they unite in their desire to kill me, I know their secret. They think I am going to tell.

The woman marrying the man wears white and red for her wedding dress, and the woman losing the man is dressed in bridesmaid pink. She is having her dress fitted, we are discussing last ditch efforts. The wedding is drawing close; she is starting to give up. She is bitter. They trap me in a tower with a metal spiral staircase. They seal me in and intend to flood the tower, but I escape through a window and manage to climb by ivy and stone and scraped knees down into the garden.

I cannot afford their artifacts anyway, I think to myself as I run away from the manor. It is only by cunning and climbing that I will be able to stay alive.

I am just a girl then, with colorful mismatched clothes, running through the garden

And then,

Sitting at my desk, looking at the landscape of my office, surveying the territory. A time comes when you stop making space, and work within the space you have created. Sensing in all directions the shape of what is by indicating what isn't, knowing all the while these specified boundaries will transform. Towers collapsing and whatnot.

The cowgirl in me rides the range. From the point of view of emptiness, there is no difference between a deity and dog shit (when the dalai lama tells this story, he says "sprout"). But from the point of view of the object perceiving emptiness, there is one hell of a difference.

Yeah buddy, you best believe it. A very big difference indeed. Indicating these boundaries can be very important. Drawing these lines, where the writing comes from. Indicating this and that, opening the well. Where the writing comes from, inviting you in, and now seeing you in my mirrors, in the steam on the glass of my shower door, in the rearview when I'm driving at night. Where it does come in, mist creeping through the open window, even with the curtains drawn.

WOLF I cry DON'T BOTHER TO HIDE YOUR WOLF'S EYES

And then,

Deep breath, plunge, *āvatāra*, bringing about descent, entering into. The boat drifts away from the shore, the tether slipping loosely from its ring, rope uncoiling. A shush, a breath of dust, and then gone, trailing uselessly into the water. Gone beyond, set apart, set adrift.

Drifting, gently lapping, creaking. Crickets, dark moon, strange light, stars. Gentle and persistent currents, rocking, spinning. It goes unnoticed, shallow at first. But the shore drops away quickly, then shelf, then abyss. Deep things move slowly below, huge and with certainty. Further away from the shore than close now. Land dissolves, a thing of the past, no where, no thing.

Drifting between above and below. Horizon becomes irrelevant as vertices assert themselves. Slowing, stopping: sinking. The caressing of ankles with foam, the backs of knees, salt lapping over thighs. A deep breath, and then submersion.

The closing of sound, the muffled aches of a different orchestra. Heartbeats and bubbles, refraction of light. The sky grows further away, dark light streaks through expanding fathoms. Further away than close to the surface now. Streaming hair, grasses, fingers.

Mountain tops, ridges appear, grottoes. Turning into the descent now, the shape of the deep just seen in the failing light, humbling vastness, quickening darkness. Faces of buildings of rocks and coral, structures, cultures, deeply buried ancient civilization.

Light and shadow dancing, a leviathan passes above where once was down. Massive body undulates overhead, generating substantive waves that propel, push, urge, overcome. Showing no resistance, effortlessly deeper. The leviathan takes the last of the light.

Shifting veils of blue on blue, bluest, black. Currents of unseen things blowing winds of deepening distance. Dark curtains part

And then,

Turning the page of the book. A line is drawn. And then another. And another, this and that. And another, self and other, just enough to maybe scratch out a name.

Dick and Jane walk to school in bobby socks holding sexless hands. Impotent cherubs in smart new uniforms, they are defined by the red of their flesh, despite the white of their identical insides. Forms and emptiness, figures in motion, ignorant of the shifting ocean tides around them. On the next page, a man appears laughing, graphite face, beard heavy strokes.

The page turns again and geometry appears, the calculus of mudrā. Tracings of hands and gestures create precise masks meant to be worn. My mask is a rabbit. As I look at it, the wolves draw near. I look at them and hold it up, look at them through my mask. They look at me, they see my face

And then,

I am a rabbit.
Thundering heart and silent feet.
Ragged stench of broken grass underfoot
tearing breath in burning lungfuls.

I am sharp with fear, fully amplified
Thudding bright and narrow
focus and speed, the beam
of the moon filling wells of eyes.

I am driven, pursued
by maddening lust,
salivating long jaws grinning.

I duck and cover
turn into hiding
a sidelong burrow and
for many moonlit minutes
study the face of the beast.
The beast now still
seeking me, smelling for me,
rooting.

The shape, the eyes,
the thrust of this
Almost companion.

The body tenses as my defenses
are penetrated,
I am perceived and pursued again

And then,

I am in my grandmother's basement, this time with my sister. I get the feeling that it is the middle of night, and we are not supposed to be awake. She is sitting on the couch with her arms around her knees.

I'll be right back, I tell her, and walk toward the back of the house, the unfinished part of the basement. Bed sheets hang from laundry line tied to floor joists overhead, veils of damp linen. Dollhouses are set up for play next to shelves of empty glass Ball jars. Passing the door to grandpa's stained glass workshop, I see a hallway, a door never noticed before.

I go slow. I've learned to be mindful of doors in dreams. It is a plain wooden door, cheap, hollow core. It has a simple knob. The hallway was dark, but the door seems somehow lighted. I am assessing the door and about to reach for the handle when I feel presence behind me. No sound, not yet, just feeling someone or something approaching behind me. Senses sharpen, prickle, listen. Yes, there. I can hear breathing now. Any moment whatever it is will be upon me.

In situations like this, the instinct is to run. I've had plenty of dreams where I've given chase, fleeing unseen dangers, terrors, nameless horror. Dark men, mad women, lurching contorted beasts. Sometimes, running like hell is the best option. But when I have enough clarity and presence, I try to face these fears, get a good look at them.

Breathe deeply. Close my eyes and conjure up fierce visions of the most horrific monsters I can think of, all the wrathful emanations. I listen, listen, wait until just the right moment, I turn, and then

Are you okay? asks the father figure, looking down the hallway. I cannot see his features, only a silhouette. What are you doing here? You know you're not supposed to be here.

I recover quickly from my surprise and move toward him, begin my habitual apology, explanation already pouring from my tongue. I'm not doing anything, I just, I thought I heard something, placating, completing the formula. Walking away, looking once more at the unopened door.

You're not supposed to go in there, I think to myself. That's where they keep the mother under the floorboards

And then,

Victorian houses are falling in on themselves impossibly, imploding. I am in a courtyard near one such house. I see other students milling about, and I remember having been here before, a kind of garden. I feel undefined sadness at coming here again, I've been here before, this is some kind of story into which I'm walking.

Inside the broken protection of the fallen house, I see my family. They are bedding down for the night, but I won't be staying there with them. I hug each of them in turn: my mother and father, my sister, my grandparents, and Mere Ruth is there also. I tuck them in and kiss them goodnight.

Wandering out into the dusk, I find a notebook left in the corner of the courtyard, from the last time I dreamed this dream. It has a picture of a cat in it, and a story about a remarkable boy who had somehow continued his lineage, propagated some sort of beastly crossing. I saw him, the boy, he was growing. Magical, beastly pearls, I think, and then I see the procession that follows him.

Very elaborate, very dogmatic, trumpets of pomp and circumstance. Fine silks and gilded brocade. Ticker tape offerings, jars of wine and cymbals crashing, and then the princesses come. I am walking behind them, the unseen queen. They wear finely tailored gowns, green and blue and gold. The backs of their gowns are cut deeply and hang like garlands to the hip, revealing their spines, shoulder blades.

Each girl carries eggs under her skin, one egg on each shoulder blade. They are grotesque and beautiful, stretched skin scaly, opalescent with pearls. Almost lizard like, the large heavy eggs under stretched skin look like stunted sprouts of wings. I follow behind and watch them, object of celebration, all this opulence.

My simple white gown drifts behind like a cloud. I am silent.

The procession rounds the corner of the imploding house. I can not see it, but something happens, music turns to screams and wails and banners fall to the ground. Everywhere it comes apart, the participants scattered, finery underfoot, I know I have to get to the king, find out what is happening. As I am running toward the source of chaos, everyone else is running away, girls with deflated and useless flaps of skin, torn dresses, broken strings of pearls.

I turn the corner and the king is lying on the ground, a small circle, onlookers. No one touches him, no one speaks to him. He is mortally wounded. His red leather armor, once grand, now has a deep crater in the chest, where his heart had been. There is blood and death everywhere, I am watching the whole mad procession collapse.

I kneel at his side, blood soaking my white dress. He clutches at me and says, You have to take me into you, and as I consider this I notice my hands are shaking. My hands are shaking and it is the sound of violins, winding up and up, spiraling into sustained echoes, my hands are vibrating to the frequency of the violins and I realize that I'm hearing my own scream, vibrating to the sound of my own scream and I wake with my hands still shaking

And then,

There is an explainer, an excuser, one who gives reasons. An apologist.

In the middle of all that self-deprecation, an objection comes. Make no apologies. Fearlessness, divine pride.

And then a clear, quiet voice appears, and resolves the tension between the two.

Fear manifests again in a different guise, this time with more aggression. Another cycle, another tension, another resolve. And then again, more subtly now:

No one will ever read this.
No one wants to hear this.
You will die alone
and no one will remember you.

despair
and then,
clear, calm, certain:

remember who?

And then,

Inviting in, what I am, what am I. Parting my curtains for you. Partaking, the cup set before me, wearing that dress. Because this isn't about me, not really, it is about the interdependence of things. The re-entrant loops, reciprocal nets. Sub-nets within wider nets, expression rather than sublimation.

What I am, fingers on the keys. Hands on the steering wheel. What am I, walking down the concourse. Terrible loneliness in public, public all around us. It is, after all, a shiny apple. Go ahead and use what's left of the curse. You know who you are.

It is why desire writes so well. Like walking from one climate to another. By the time you realize you've gone too far and don't have a coat, you are farther from home than close to it. Like going out on a lake and not realizing how far you've paddled, alone. This is what it is like to write about desire.

Ways unfed desire opens earliness/ takes us to the root of conflict/ shows us the root of conflict/ shows us the structure of the conflict we intimately are

And then,

There is a garden. It is circular in shape, defined by low and exquisitely composed hedges. The hedges are waist high and form a path suitable for a person to walk comfortably, but passing another person being will require contact.

There appears to be no one here. Looking across the top of the ornate pattern of hedges, there is a tree in the center of the garden. Can't make it out clearly, but it seems to unfurl above the hedge, stretching and twisting, ropy branches and dense, lush leaves. Looking at the tree and trying to estimate the distance, finding my calculations useless. This appears to be labyrinth, no telling how the journey will be, what will be encountered here.

Approaching the entrance, the only way forward. Going backward means leaving this place. Looking at the tree again, sizing it up, and entering. Taking up a business-like pace, neutral and perfunctory, making my way into the hedges. The ground feels firm beneath my feet, trying to follow the shape of the turns I'm taking, make an image of this path. Seeking a sense of trajectory, the shape of this pattern I'm traversing, not long at all and I've lost all sense, just moving forward. Relation to the tree transforms over time. It remains equidistant for many turns, and then suddenly appears to draw near, only to dance away again.

I grow bored: begin to study the shape of the hedges themselves, the texture of the leaves. Although they only grow waist high, they would be difficult to cross. They are wide and thick with thorns. They are intended, trained to tangles concealed beneath the lush leaves. I grow cold: someone or something made them this way, nurtured this.

I stop. Look back toward the entrance, and then again at the tree. Between the center and the edge now, looking at the shape of the whole. Motion appears in the periphery of my vision and I see a figure then, bare-chested, making way through the labyrinth.

Ducking instantly, scared of shadow, go to ground, catch my breath. Won't go back, I am meant to go to that tree. I will not crawl the rest of the way there just to remain unseen by this stranger. Peeking over the edge of the hedge, my heart stops: there will be no hiding. The figure is standing still now, looking directly at me, grinning. Smelling me. My heart thuds, slowing, standing, fixed in headlights. We see each other clearly, grinning with anticipation and fear, naked-waisted.

Long minutes eye gazing. A step forward. And another. Then another, and we are off, moving the same matched pace, never straying. Exchanging gait and gaze and noticing the pace increasing. Something in the grinning, lolling gleam that causes fingers of thrill.

Ever quickening now. Turns become tighter, loops and shimmies and figure eights. Don't hurry, savoring. Drawing close, seeing the shape, hearing the breathing. In counterpoint we cross from open sky to being under the canopy of the tree, passing through a veil of coiling perfume and vines. Looking ahead, seeing the intimate mosses, the fruit growing there. And then we are met, we and the tree. The tree uncoils, offers fruit, and I accept and take it in my left hand.

Don't do it, he says. Devouring me with his eyes, watching my every move. Don't you dare, he grins.

Wolf, I say. Smiling. Holding the fruit.

If you eat that, it means you're a bad girl, he says, stepping closer. Touching my hair, withdrawing. Smell of him, smell of sun and wind. Out of the hedges now, naked, vulnerable. I am holding the fruit, this is my garden, my tree, my fruit.

Is that so? I ask him. Holding the fruit. Fingers trembling, daring to touch my face, my lips.

A very bad girl, he says, salivating. Closer still, standing close and clear, inches apart, not touching. Horripilating, ripening.

If you put that in your mouth, we will have to dance this dance all over again, he grins. He touches my breasts then, sighs, hefts and caresses them. I am looking at the fruit in my hand, squeezing. He inhales deeply at my neck, nuzzles, noses at my openings. Feeling the shape and direction of him, the quality of his energy.

Who are you, I ask.

Stop being such a doubting thomas, he nibbles. You know I will be who you need me to be. The important thing, what you have to tell me: who are you?

Fingers in the small of my back, winding the key there. I feel the rippling, the intermingling tides, the resonant frequency in response to intent, aspiration.

Touch me in a way that pleases me, I say, and I will show you. Mouths close, shared breath, lifted fruit and faces. Lick the skin. Moans, staring. Irresistible tongue, teeth and skin and biting and kisses. Juices, flesh, tasted

And then,

I am looking at you.

I visualize you clearly. I see the curve of your mouth.

I see the corner of your eye, how it is.

I see you.

I catch a glimpse,

peripheral vision

of all of you, your greatness

seeing you precisely as you are.

You are beautiful,

and I love you,

and I am deep with gratitude

at the sight of you

And then,

I am putting up my winter clothes and wishing I am gone, going home, folding sweaters to stack on shelves. As I put them away overhead I notice a little door, maybe a cabinet never seen before. I touch the knob, soft and round, remembering I did open this door once, looking for teeth I had lost. Remembering being here before, there's some kind of trick, otherwise the door is too small. Impossibly small. I could maybe get my head and one shoulder through. Certainly, if I can get both shoulders through, I'll just slide right in, and ah, yes. That's how to get through. Relief after panic, remembering the trick is not to panic.

The dream consists of many doorways like this, one after another. In every scene, each reality offers such a door, visible if I do not panic. Dozens of different times and places, all kinds of realities. From time to time, I run into people I know, doing whatever it is they happen to be doing that lifetime. Many absurdities open, like the room full of babies, crawling around on big red and blue blocks that were hard and soft at the same time. I hurry out of that one, panic rising, and find myself on a boat, the waves are huge and gray. Someone I know is tugging on the rigging. Crawling through a porthole, opening a panel, and then

I fall out of a sarcophagus, a monument, of a man on a horse with a sword. I fall out of the base into a public park at nighttime. The grass is soft and lushly green, crickets, and I gaze up at the statue of the notable somebody astride a horse. There is a man in a bright moonlit suit and a fancy hat standing there, looking down at me. Other people trail behind him, following his lead. They appear to be waiting for me.

I want the keys you have, he says. I stand up and dust off my ass, the knees of my jeans. I will make a trade with you, he says.

Too rattled by the ship babies and the awkward doors, I don't even ask for his name. I have a sense of the interlocking boxes I've just been moving through. He sees my skepticism and gestures toward a body of water nearby. We walk together, his people trailing behind. I can tell they have come from here and are reluctant to return.

I will take your keys in exchange for this submarine, he says.

I almost quip, Is it yellow? and decide that this would be the wrong thing to say, looking at his people.

This submarine functions in the same way as your horse, he says, but the movement is different, more fluid. I feel some anxiety. I was just getting comfortable with the gait of the whole trap-door thing, and now a submarine. All that water! But I trade my keys anyway, climb inside

And then,

I am in my bed, sleeping. Or at least, doing my best full-body impression of sleeping. I hold the big pillow against the length of my body, right arm tucked around, knee drawn up. This is how I learned how to not sleep with a teddy bear: I got a bear of a pillow. The covers are tucked between my legs, keeping my feet cool. This is how I know when insomnia will strike: my feet get dry and hot. Almost unbearably so, and I hang them out the covers to cool them.

My left arm is under my pillow, supporting my head, and my fingers dangle over the edge of the mattress. When I was younger, this was impossible to do, no hands or feet could cross that protective border. It was an unspoken magic formula: on the bed and under the blanket is safe. Anything that crosses outside of that circle is fair game.

I have struck a balance now, and so am drifting between asleep and awake. Wandering through thoughts of the day. Grocery list. What to wear to the office tomorrow. Wandering, drifting, and where my hand is hanging over the edge of the bed my fingers begin to tingle. They become vague, undefined.

More space between thoughts now, tension seeping out of muscles into the mattress, dripping and disappearing into the floor. More space, and other sounds and images start to come, the sensation in my fingers spreading to other parts of my body. I am seeing. Not literal shapes at first, just impressions, snatches of conversation. Like listening into the wind, or to people sitting at other tables next to you in a crowded restaurant. Tuning into different messages, different sense impressions.

I try not to get too excited, pop the bubble. I also try not to become too lax, drift all the way into automated sleep cycles. This is tricky. Disconnected words, pictures, feelings parade. Some are enticing, and I want to follow them. Some are frightening, and I want to look away.

I just watch, I just breathe, I just attend to them all equally and then

I am standing in a garden.

It is a low garden, it does not appear meant to impress anybody. Hedges, calf high. There might be an ocean nearby. A warm breeze.

At my feet a red feather. A cardinal feather, sitting on orange-brick cobblestone. Reaching down for it, turning in my fingers. Holding the quill precisely with my thumb and forefinger, I walk down the path to the gate with the big red doors.

Huge red doors, immense. At once shiny and slick, slightly textured, patent red doors. Rounded, arching, interwoven somehow. Complex locking mechanism. The door's odd angles and interconnected parts all meet and are held in the center by a large, oddly shaped lock. I peer, I wonder, I shrug. What else can I do? I reach up and very lightly, very softly, tickle the lock with my feather.

The breeze stirs. A sigh. I look closer at my feather. It has a strong, flexible spine, and soft color. Stepping closer with more confidence, I run the pliant tip of the feather over the strange, bulbous shapes of the lock, its ridges and folds and ropy intersections.

Where the feather caresses, the skin of the lock begins to shift and separate, reaching into limbs. The touch of the feather causes ripples of motion in the door, the awakening of hands and legs and knees and arms twisting in on themselves, grasping, clutching. A rolling boil of bodies, trunks turning, growing larger out of the leathery shifting skin of the door. The red door is alive.

I step back suddenly, pulling the feather away. The door cries out in anguish, sighs of disappointment. The body made of bodies itself, beautiful and terrifying, writhing. Watching the door perpetuate itself, procreate, waste no time planting seeds for the next emanation. Skin and fluid motion intercoursing through interconnected strands of limbs, scissor legs. Dozens of key locks where the door meets together, opening and closing.

What do I have to do, I think. Looking at the door, the frame. I notice a koi pond to the left of the door, cool blue water in all this hot flesh, take a deep breath and another step back. Red door, red feather, the red door in the south

I gasp I think I know where I am

And then lifting the feather up to the door again, touching the centermost union. Just there, on just the right spot, gently and firmly, slowly at first but with steadily increasing attention. The door escalates, vibrates with pleasure, and then crests into laughter and delight. All of the muscles relaxing, the door falls away, and the red gate, the one in the south, opens. I go inside.

In the courtyard, I have the impression of beasts. Weird tusks, bristly hair, elephantine. There are animals tethered to a cart which I later perceive as horses. Still orange-red cobblestones, but now the gardens are far more resplendent, dewy. Dripping with honey. It is very thick, this garden, full of very sticky things that smell wonderful.

I keep moving, not wanting to become intoxicated, all that nectar. There are steps, and as I ascend I see the full resplendent nature of the courtyard, the blue sky, the banners. I focus, I must focus and the front doors are opening wide, grandly, as the doors of such places do.

Inside is a lovely hall, an entryway. A huge crystal chandelier refracting light, tinkling. There are people here, dressed in their finest, talking about fine things. They are beautiful people and they are loving the fine things, loving each other. They all look similar somehow, they all belong here. I flutter, worried they will see me, want to talk to me, ask me questions.

They are loving each other and the fine things, and glass is tinkling, and soft laughter is soaked up by the wallpaper. The wallpaper in this hallway of parlours is extraordinary, as is the pattern on the carpet. Gorgeous looping vines, patterns of stripes and flowers that look remarkably like the pattern on the red door. I watch the pattern undulate with increasing ecstasy, and will myself to look away. I don't have anything to say here. Where was I going? Not these rooms, not these conversations. There's somewhere I'm supposed to be.

Trying to remember, keep going. I am in the hallway, I have made steps down the long hallway. The debutantes become gray and less distinct as I walk away, I am in the hallway, there is a staircase not far from here, just past the table, I am approaching the steps with the door at the top when sleep washes out the color

And then,

Sub-basement of a factory, catacombs, machinery, brick and mortar tomb. Weak naked lightbulbs feed huge shadows through crumbling archways. I am passing through different rooms separated by these archways, yawning and choked with spider webs. The floor is wet and dark, gritty footsteps echo.

Becoming aware this is a meat factory. The walls are hung with corpses, meat hooks, other instruments of slaughter, torture porn. The dripping wet sticky is blood. Recognition blooms in me with deep horror, and as the feeling unfolds I pass through an archway into a room housing immense meat grinders.

Gargantuan replicas of old fashioned meat grinders, like you might find at a butcher. Meat is pushed into one end, and a crank of the wheel passes it out the other side, spilling blood and pulp and minced bones and whatever else you please. These grinders have an automated conveyor belt dumping live meat into the grinder's funnel. I see myself there, among other people and animals. Pigs are milling about, and people I don't know, and people I do know. I observe the sense of swine on the conveyor belt, meat for the slaughter, unknowing.

I watch us all lined up on our way to the meat grinder, slowly progressing toward the end of the conveyor belt, but I am talking and laughing with my family, completely unmoved and unaware of impending death. I am looking into the maw of the machine, the gore pouring from the other end, the idiot smell of meat, the happy faces of my family.

Crying out at the atrocity from the belt and from where I observe the scene simultaneously, a wailing erupts from my chest and denies the whole image, and the dream dissolves. It breaks apart, it melts away, and my anguish is washed over by warm and cool light, creamy comfort, soothing. My vision is filled with chenrezig, brilliant and shining.

S/he smiles at me, a wind perfumed with flowers, without words I am reassured. I wake briefly, breathe deep, and sink into a dreamless sleep

And then,

I am sitting at the kitchen table, looking at a picture of a woman who gave birth to my fathers. My grandfathers, even. The woman who fathered my lineage.

My mom hands me the photograph over piles of memorabilia she dug out from the attic, leftovers from my great hermit uncle, Sam. An illustrated program from the World's Fair, the Wonders of Tomorrow, so many lifetimes ago. A TimeLife magazine full of darling advertisements for the latest and greatest, tonics and snake oils, cosmic debris. A crumbling letter from an unknown woman, describing to my uncle away at war about the rifle accident.

And then this photograph, printed on cardstock, thick soft edges. Water stained, sweat, this image of a little girl who is me. Our likeness is uncanny.

When I saw this, I jumped, my mother says. I saw you there, she looks just like you at that age. My baby.

I am looking up at myself from the photograph very seriously. In the picture, I am buttoned into a woolen suit and pleated skirt, no more than three or five years of age. Immobilized by layers of clothing, corseted into a thick weave that has big anchors embroidered on the lapel. In the sepia of the photograph there's no telling the color of the anchors, imagining them as white. Bright, on dark blue or red maybe, nothing too fancy. My knee boots are well worn, not evenly laced. Big hooks and buttons anchor the suit, pleats and all, to my body. My uniform.

I am propped up in the picture, a stuffed doll, on several bales of hay. It appears as though the photograph was taken outdoors, but the background perspective is all wrong. I am staged in this photograph, still. Proper. Seen, not heard.

Turning the card over, the print says:

> Carpenter & Hover,
> Scenic & Portrait Photographers
> Views of all Popular Scenery in This Vicinity.
> *Negatives retained for future orders*

Many flourishes embellish this text, elaborate vine-laden illustrations: a box camera, and an easel, some roses and lilies, bluebells and cattails and a tiny drawing of a beach with sailboats. I see an urn, and a photo album, and other decorative elements. Guessing, it comes from a time of waistcoats and corsets, and other complex restrictions on creativity.

Can I have this, Mom, I ask.

Negatives retained for future orders, the card says, implying a future. Sitting the picture on my desk at home, I stare into the face of this little girl, this woman who must have given birth to one of my fathers some generations ago. Her face has the features I've inherited from my father: a shape to the intersection of eyes and nose, the bridge of his face that is my face. I have those eyes and nose, my father has them. She has them, this grandmother.

This old photograph. One hundred years old, maybe? All of the hands that touched her over the years. I feel something hard in her gaze, wonder if I'm seeing my reflection. Her beautiful eyes, contradictions, appearing at once sad and angry, then blank and dull. Round face, short baby hair, though her mother did curl the ends.

My other grandmother's house, where giant heavy-framed portraits of my sister and me used to hang, dressed in our Sunday best. Pictured together, seated demurely in my red and white polka-dot dress, a soft book about a turtle clutched in my hand. Fidgeting when Mom curled my hair, causing a searing burn on my forehead. The photographer doesn't believe me when I tell him, I am done reading this book, can I please have another.

My ancestor, we share this in common: we do not appear to enjoy the dog and pony show, this dressing up for propriety. Doing what a lady does, just because that's how we've always done it. Anchors and buckles, straps and restraints, pleats and polka-dots.

Looking at this photograph, imagining, simulating, a connection opening up between me and this grandmother. A tiny doorway opens and a story grows about what her life is like, what it feels like to wear that dress. Knowing her smile by feel, mirror face.

Interdependent existence, a thread contributing to this storied lineage, this is her story as much as it is my story

And then,

I am walking with a companion through the dusk drenched streets of La Jolla. Full of good food and wine, window shopping. Here are awful expensive clothes I'd never wear, even if I could afford them. Here are bright and beautiful diamonds, gemstones, worth more than we'll ever make. Nose to windows, marveling, pondering, imagining who would wear such jewels.

I do not see the older woman approach. She is suddenly standing beside me, speaking, gazing through the window. These are beautiful stones, she says. But they are set so poorly. She has silver hair, silver bangles, she is sturdy and certain in her movement.

See, they just don't know how to set stones in this country, she goes on. Sometimes they're right overseas, but these are nothing like that. It doesn't matter how many facets you've cut in the stone if the setting isn't right, if it doesn't bring the light. If the setting isn't right, the diamond won't shine.

I don't know anything about that, I say, I'm just daydreaming. She clucks her tongue at the window, at me, is walking away

And then,

I hear her calling to me. Come in, Miss Model, we're ready for you. The room is dim, big easels and desks arranged in a loose circle around a platform. The track lighting is arranged to spot the platform, bright enough that the spillover provides illumination for the twelve odd artists in a loose circle around the room. I enter silently, approach the circle.

Right up here, dearie, the instructor says. You can put your robe there, she says, Now let me know if you get cold, we can turn the air conditioning off if you get cold there.

I nod, smile. I step into the circle, into the light. I can not see the faces looking at me, trying not to look. I set my bag on the floor, I loosen my robe.

We'll do eight minutes she says, and then a change, eight minutes, and then a change, until the break. Try not to take positions where you'll get tired easily. If you feel something start to get numb, just shake it out and go back to position. After the break we'll try using a sheet, too.

I nod, smile. Breathe, heart pounding, and then take off my robe. Drop it, find a place to make a stand. Eight minute statue for seven bucks an hour, that's me. Maybe music is playing. I can't see any of the artists' faces, but I can hear the pens and pencils. This is life drawing two, and I am life, being drawn. I focus on my breathing and feel the air against my skin, the energy of twelve pairs of eyes translating me to paper.

Occasionally the art woman, the instructor makes comments or talks at me. She never uses my name in front of the other students, but instead introduces me to the class as Miss Model, as if they don't already know me. There are others that alternate classes with me, a Mr. Model and at least one other Miss Model. We are the subjects of the drawing, the objects of practice.

Long, silent minutes in stillness, standing. I can feel the curves of my hips being traced, the underside of my arm. Chills and beads of sweat, halogen glare. Silent faces scratching broad heavy strokes on oversized paper, breathing, rustling, breathing, scratching. Half-way through class we get a break. I go outside to smoke a cigarette, as do many of the artists. Crouched on the curb in my robe, surrounded by witnesses of my nakedness, different in sunlight somehow. The boy next to me scuffs his sneakers in the sand. Is that hard for you, to stand there like that? he asks. I smile, I exhale, Sometimes, I say.

I put my arms over my head and cup my elbows, hair pouring down over my shoulders, my breasts, my shoulder blades. Oh, don't do it Miss Model, your arms will go numb, says the art matron.

I'll be okay, I say, and settle myself firmly on my feet, seventy thirty, tai chi style.

Suit yourself, she says, and begins her slow perimeter walk of the easels. Hawk eyes, she peers over shoulders, peers at me, sights me, tries to see me the way the student intends to show me. I can't always hear the conversation. Still and breathing slow, I feel the light and heavy attention of shape and form, drawings coming forth.

My mind wanders. As my muscles grow tired, I start to fret. Eight minutes is a very long time, sometimes. Aware of the full geography of my feet, all the ways weight gets distributed. Increasingly aware of the sensation of air on skin, especially the parts usually concealed. Painfully aware of facial muscles, even though only three students can see my face at a time.

Questions of scale and symbol scroll through my mind, studying the patterns of the stucco on the wall, the glow of the red exit sign. I wonder periodically if I will survive. I contemplate if I will ever regret this experiment, and decide it must be unlikely, because at least it will make an interesting story.

After class is over, the she-teacher sends all of the artists from the room. In the dark, she turns to me and says, Okay, Miss Model. You get to look at them first. Let me know when you're done and I will come and grade them. Then the students will pack up. And she leaves.

Barefoot, I step outside of the ring of easels and light, and make my way around the room. I see twelve different versions of me, twelve facets of appearance through the eyes and skill of twelve different artists.

Portraits of self through the eyes of others, my stillness reflected through them, twelve different mirrors. I walk the circle and feel a rainbow of emotion. Intense discomfort, unexpected pleasure, humble and grateful for the art I am helping to create. Tears spring to my eyes, willing subject

And then,

I am in a general store, maybe a pharmacy. It is nighttime, and the fluorescent lights are hard as the linoleum floor. Either my sister is there, or I am supposed to be buying something for her, maybe some make-up. Walking up and down the aisles, looking. I turn a corner and am by the front door, automatic sliding glass panels.

Outside the door, a wolf is in the parking lot, cantering. As I walk through, the doors shush open and we are off, loping. I follow the wolf across the suburban nightscape, my sister forgotten. We rise through scrubland, it is hard to keep up, but running feels so good. And then I am climbing a sandy slope, very steep, very difficult to ascend, like swimming upriver through earth. It requires concentration.

At the top of the hill I am panting, it is narrow, not very wide across. There is a depression in the sand, a perfectly shaped hollow under some brush, I am crawling in and remembering this place I made for myself. Yes, I can be just like this, and the hill will hold me gently. I feel around, I think I left a pack of cigarettes here, yes, ah.

Looking, smoking, remembering. All around, little mounds, little cairns, memories, totems. Dozens close by, older stretching off down the hill. Smiling, will have to go soon, happy to be here now and smoke this cigarette

And then,

I am on a bus, somehow sleeping on the floor between the seats. A day that opened with possibility closes too soon, like any other day, a day that sought greatness and settled for normalcy. Normalcy is miraculous, what a rare gem, everything is normal, A-OK. Dusky, husky, too many cigarettes the night before. I feel the rumble of the road, snaked down between seats. I am sleeping underneath the seat of someone I don't know, sprawled above me. I chose to sleep on the floor nearby, because I liked something, a look in the face.

Older than my years, younger than my heart. The engine drones out all other sound as the light ebbs away. I keep a sweater as a blanket, tuck my legs under. I am on the bus, I have always been on the bus, really. I started out on the bus, and no matter how many times I get off I get back on again. The next somewhere, here I am, there I go, here we go again.

The stranger snores and rolls, arm hangs down, over the side of the seat. Fingers hang inches above my chest, and I think about when I was a little girl, how I used to worry about my limbs over the edge of the bed. With every bump of the bus over the road fingertips graze the hilltops of my sweater, felt informally, unconsciously. Hold me closer, tiny dancer.

I don't know what power is, which makes me a perfect vessel for power. I wouldn't know power if it stamped itself on my forehead, if I came emblazoned with authority tattooed on every inch of my skin. Power uses me sometimes, I am power-full. I cannot see power when it wraps its fingers in my hair, bites my neck. I cannot see power when I am full up with it, when I am doubled over in my yielding. Have I always been this way? An empty vessel. I practice openness, I go the way of water, I lay myself low. All the way to the floor of the bus, where I can see the shoes and socks of all the other passengers. The floor is a black, rubberized material. I have a backpack for a pillow.

My nipples are getting hard. I breathe deeply, try and offer up a little more flesh to those maybe sleeping fingers, those maybe perfectly aware of what they're doing fingers. The bus jumps and so do I, giving over to the fantasy: I imagine that rather than sleeping, there is intention in the action of my companion. Knowing the subtle opportunity given, knowing I choose to lie down on the floor of the bus here, under. In view of everyone, an open secret, knowing touching this way in full view of other passengers.

Taking advantage of this opportunity, titillating. I pretend this is true, and my body responds to my mental life, nipples now like little diamonds under my sweater. My eyes are closed, I am perspiring. Will anyone notice that I'm intentionally not noticing fingers grazing the pasture of my young body? I laugh at myself, grinning chuckle.

The other passengers are sleeping, as well. The bus is silent, except for the groan of the motor under my hips, my buttocks, my shoulder blades. I am alone on the bus, I think, maybe. I will always be on the bus, somehow, always ready to see how the show unfolds, always ready to rise to the pleasure of the *lila*, the great play. Vowing to take rebirth until all sentient beings are liberated.

As a woman, I think to myself, diamond goose bumps. I vow to take rebirth as a woman

And then,

I go outside to smoke a cigarette. Smoking is allowed inside the bar, but it is summer dusk and the earliest nightcrawlers are creeping into the sidewalks and sidelines, scoping the scene. I guess that makes me one of them.

I sit in the chair with my legs crossed, smoking and watching and smiling. A woman comes down the sidewalk, I hear her shiffling feet approach. Older, frizzy hair, slippered feet. She wears a tired housedress and clutches her purse in her hands, arms folded up tight to her chest. Trying to look and not look, she passes and I feel a moment of panic, she might see me seeing her. Our eyes meet for a flash and then she is shuffling with her back to me, turning into the convenience store on the corner. I smoke a sigh of relief and promptly forget her, return to my observation at a distance.

Startled when she shuffles before me again, now framed by the circle of a lonely streetlight. She is looking at me, I smile my smile. Hi, I say.

It looks really bad, doesn't it, she asks me. Her hands are fluttering, clutching at her purse.

Excuse me, I say, feeling my stomach mirror her hands. I can see by the movement of her body, her eyes that she is used to having lots of conversations at once with maybe not always people. Crazy cat-lady, for sure.

Her eyes focus on mine and she smiles. Her hands flutter: first to her mouth with a cigarette, then to her eye, then cresting wisps of hair at the crown of her head. Black eye, she says. The guy in there, when I was buying smokes, he said it was really bad this time, looks just terrible. He said, Honey you don't look so good.

Looking at her face, seeing the thinness of skin, fragility of aging beauty, perpetually half-dead. It's not that bad, I say hopefully, and she smiles again, flutters.

Thank you darlin', you're a sweetie, she laughs through a cloud of smoke. I fell down the stairs, I swear, she says, vamping. Her hands, still for a moment, jump up again to her eye, a welting dark blossom of broken blood vessels. It looks like she's forgotten to put on the smoky-shadow eye make-up on half of her face.

You could always put some purple eye shadow on the other eye, I say. It occurs to me, hearing these words I'm speaking, that this is a horrible thing I have just said. How grotesque that it is possible to say something like that, this is the most I have to offer this woman. This stranger, somebody or other's mother, maybe.

It turns out to be enough. She smiles, for real this time, genuine. I was too old for that years ago, she says, and laughs again. She shuffles from one foot to the other, and then her feet are walking, her hands are fluttering, and she is wandering away. She goes and I breathe again, watch her turn down some unseen side street

And then,

I am standing at the front counter. What do you want your name to be? she asks, chewing on the end of her pen.

Um, I don't know, I shrug, trying not to stare at the products and advertisements on the wall. I didn't know I had to have a name, actually.

Oh, you have to, we don't use our real names here, the Spanish speaking one says to me. Propped up on the counter, she pouts her lips very seriously. She has curly hair, and glittery glue-on eyelashes. My name is Estrella, she says.

The dominatrix, the one who runs the staff, says What kind of shoe are you wearing?

I look at the chunky, strappy, obscenely high heels I've purchased for this job. What do you mean? I ask her, and my pulse quickens. Should I know something special about shoes?

You know, she says, the name of your shoe. She rolls her eyes at me, Like the brand. She flips her ponytail impatiently.

To others I seem dull and slow. I didn't know. I slid a shoe off my foot and read MIA. Missing in action? Mia, I say.

Mia, you look like a Mia okay, she says. You'll be Mia, that's how I'll write it on the schedule, and that's what the boys up front will know you by.

Okay, I say, nodding to show I understand. Estrella beams at me. Mia, she says.

And then I have been working in the shop for three weeks, two shifts a week. Our shifts are six to eight hours, overlapping with one other girl so we don't have to be alone the whole time. I have Friday nights and Sunday mornings.

We are lingerie models, and sit on a raised platform in the back of the store. Each girl gets to pick her own outfit, her own music. There are strict rules for a private showing of the lingerie. The model stays on the stage, the patron sits in the chair. There are limits on what can be revealed. No touching. Cash only plus tips, watch for twenty minutes.

In all the rooms there are timers and emergency buttons within reach of the dancer, spotlights and music players. Chairs for the patrons. Houseplants. Sliding panels so the staff can monitor and make sure no rules are being broken.

There is a tiny dressing room that reeks of cigarette smoke and disinfectant. Putting on my lipstick, I bump my knees against the suitcases Estrella left there in case she might have to leave home again. My other co-worker is a mother who needs to make a little more cash to pay for daycare while she's working her other job. Her husband said it was okay. We sit on the platform, reading books and smoking cigarettes to pass the time, taking turns with whoever walks through the door.

I dare myself. As a full time undergraduate student at a liberal arts college, I am a young white woman who finds herself in a heated argument about objectification of women. I am playing devils' advocate: testing the hypothesis that women who actively choose to objectify themselves become powerful. Claiming that when a woman voluntarily becomes an object of desire, she subverts the relationship of power and exerts control over the subject. Just look at Marilyn Monroe, I said. I didn't know anything about Marilyn Monroe then.

Can you do it? they ask me, I ask myself. I guess I'd better find out, I say.

This one has an English accent. Usually, I just see locals and illegal immigrants (No sex, *señor*), but this man must be a tourist. He chooses me over the housewife. I climb up on the stage and reach for the music, and he says

Wait a minute.

I stop. My feet already hurt, ready to take off my shoes. Looking at him, at ease in the chair, one leg crossed ankle to knee.

Have a seat, he says, indicating the edge of the stage. My heartbeat quickens, smiling reflexively. The emergency button is high on the wall above the stage, convenient to a dancing woman, but I will have to move fast if I sit at his feet, here. I take my utterly impractical footwear off and kick it aside.

I can't dance if I'm sitting down, I say, and smile again. I turn to the music and he stops me again.

Just for a minute, sit down. I won't keep you the whole twenty minutes, he says. He takes a fifty dollar bill from his pocket and lays it on the edge of the stage. I look at him for a long moment, I take a deep breath. I can do this I think and then,

I sit down. My legs dangle over the edge of the stage. Stocking snags as I sit, and somewhere I muse how this research in nakedness has a costly wardrobe. I cross my ankles and wait.

You're a pretty one, he says.

I look down at my knees. Smile, must smile, I smile. Thank you, I say.

I just want to look at you, talk to you for a minute, he says. You don't have to dance for me. Here, why don't you just take your top off, down to there?

His eyes dance, spotlight glare. Looking at him, imagining his home. His pets, his children. I look at the sloppy collar of his shirt, and shrug off a strap of my dress. One shoulder, he puts more money down. I shrug off the other strap.

Is this it, I think. Am I powerful now. Is he.

There, that's better, he says, and leans back. Unzips his pants, begins to find himself. Are you a student?

He asks and I am caught off guard, showing too much: eyes widen, blushing. No lying now, not directly. Yes, I say, and describe taking classes at a nearby college I do not actually attend. I'm an art student, I say.

You must be a smart artist, he says, making extra money for school here. He is looking at my legs now, between my knees. I am a rabbit. Soft heart, run fast.

You do what you have to do, you know. Leaning back on the heels of my hands, slowing. Opening, I've met some interesting people this way. He glances at my face, and then is distracted by my knees.

Oh, I bet you have, he sighs. He sits in this way for a moment, cupping chin in hand. He looks at me directly then, meeting his gaze unblinking

Spread your legs, he says. I want to see your pussy.

My heart stops. I turn away. I can't do that, I say. Absurdly: I'm sorry.

Oh, what do you mean, dear, he says softly. No need to be sorry, neither one of us. No one will know. Just show me, you don't even have to undress, I just want you to show me. I want you to do it, show me yourself. Reaching into his pocket, a fold of bills.

Show me your cunt, he says, smiling.

Deep silence. And then,

No, I reply, meeting his eyes. He stops smiling. I will lose my job, that's against the rules, I say. Another girl from my school got fired for this. As I scoot away to get up from the stage, color creeps from the collar of his wrinkled shirt.

Are you joking? he asks, A whore with a conscience? His voice starting to rise. You're not allowed to have morals, whore. He is standing up, red face spitting and I move fast now, thudding heart and feet. Opening the door wide and loud.

Get out, I say, my voice just starting to shake. Trembling. Out, or I'll get the bouncers.

Fucking cunt, fucking unbelievable, he mutters. A cunt that follows the rules, he hisses, clutching at his money.

I shut the door after him. I walk to the stage, sit down on the edge.

Did I fail. Did he.

I cry, unwilling object

And then,

I am taking a warrior stance, breathing deeply. I am in my plain room in the nunnery. It has pinkish-orange vinyl laid directly on concrete. The window is framed by iron scrollwork bars and has rare panes of glass. The window in the bathroom, on the other hand, is open to the world, high above the cold squat toilet.

Against one wall of the bedroom, a hutch holds a picture of the dalai lama and some dusty plastic flowers, plus a whole battalion of cockroaches. My roommate and I discovered these when we moved in and are deeply horrified. The very next day I go to market to buy pesticides. Any kind, the stronger the better.

Now, I am tying a bandanna around my mouth to protect me from the spray. I am holding a red and yellow can that has pictures of big, black, dead bugs on it. It is called Mo-Tox, and it is with this that I will fumigate this room.

I look like a bandit, and I'm screwed. Not only am I about to intentionally take hundreds of lives, I am about to do it in a nunnery under the nose of the dalai lama. I look at the picture of the dalai lama, the crusty flowers, and I put my can down. I put my palms together and take a deep breath. I'm sorry, I say to the image. It is going to take me a gazillion lifetimes to work this one off. I'm sorry, I'm a really long way from home and really scared. A thousand cockroaches next to my bed is just too much. Please give every single one of them rebirth in a pure land, okay?

He smiles his implacable smile. I do not find a single carcass

And then,

I climb out on the roof of the world and spread out my carpet. The winter night is very cold, but cold in the comforting way of something that will change. I spread out my carpet below me, and above me the stars blaze in space, a blanket under which I can curl with all my mortality.

Cuddled underneath stars, drawing them close to me, trying to think all the languages in which I speak star. Remembering nights in the backyard, out on the driveway, motion sickness from the spinning of the earth, all those northern hemisphere stars. Orion waves at me and I wave back, mirror image of him and the pyramids. Body, mind, stars, the law of fives. Mercury and madness and the fleetness of thought and feeling. Fragments of sentences, slices of lives.

I have a dream about snakes, about one white snake. A very white, very old, extremely venomous snake. Down in a hole with this snake, no choice about it. I am either bitten or have drunk the venom of this snake, the only antidote a red essence, some kind of emission from the tail of the snake. The outcome is uncertain but the message is clear: the poison and the cure come from the same source.

Drifting, drunk under stars. Allowing stars to romance me, dance me to the ends of space. Seduced by a black hole, us the stars, finding ourselves out past galaxies not anticipated. Light takes on new shapes and all is forgotten but the poison and the cure.

They come from the same source, those two, they come from two ends of the same snake, two sides of the same coin, two sides of the same day, two hands of the same being

And then,

The cowgirl emerges, stands before me. Even at the lowest moment she can appear. She lights her cigarette and plays a Nick Cave and Bad Seeds record, maybe Leonard Cohen or Tom Waits, a woodpecker kind of tune. She knocks her boots and doesn't apologize for the dirt that falls on the carpet. She licks her lips and grins. She strides, her boots were made for walking. This cowgirl cuts no slack. She'll do it, just because she can, especially if she shouldn't. She never second guesses, her shot is as sure as the sun, sure as the swing of a short skirt, sure as the gasp for breath that follows urging desire. She always, always shoots from the hip.

She strides into the room and my defenses falter. I am as certain as I have ever been that it is time to stay and sit a while, that I'm tired and want to sit down. Time to hang up my spurs, play it safe. Fly under the radar. And then my door swings open and there she stands, hips cocked to one side, head cocked to the other. Her skin is tan and smells like salt and sun, her face fresh with wind, her hair a hot mess. Her entire body is wind blown, she's grinning from ear to ear, she's shaking her head at me.

What in the hell is wrong with you, she laughs. She strikes a match, and I notice that her cigarettes will make the curtain smell. She is at home, everywhere. She moves freely, and worst best of all, she never ever takes no for an answer.

Wondering, wondering about the life of the cowgirl, how she makes herself at home in me. Chasing away complacency, dispelling restlessness, bound to movement, dancing. Restlessness of the sky, the natural state of being, motion like standing still. Horizon calling, sky responding, the echo of my room, my fingers, hopeless to the lilting dance.

We saddle up and before I know it I am going, going, gone. Always hearing the beckoning, whether I heed the call or not. No shape, no color, no smell or taste or sound, pulling, yearning, longing. The cowgirl laughs at me because she knows the name of that nameless beast, that mystery. The nameless is her home on the range.

She rides, and it moves her in ways I have not yet dreamed. She grits her teeth and rides hard, enjoys every saltysweet moment, borne in the sweat of her smile, the dirt under her fingernails, the soft pale glow of her thigh exposed willingly to the moonlit sky. She looks at me that way, and I'm lost. There is no defense of culture or tradition I can muster that will crack that crooked smile, that shit-eating grin. My intellectual excuses are a pale, soggy grey next to her vibrant colorful arguments.

I can't do this, I can't go with you, I have work to do I mumble, and she spits on the ground.

Who can't do this, she asks me. Where is your will? There is nothing that cannot be done, you just need to grow a pair. She smiles warmly, takes a drag off her cigarette.

Or, you could borrow mine, she grins. You know all this, I've told you before, she says. Now, what are you afraid of?

What indeed? She pitches her cigarette, glowing cherry arcing through the darkness, a comet of nicotine exploding into sparks. Burns me, leaves deft impressions, nomad nature deeply imbued in limbs. Fingers tingle, nameless tangles, drawing me out further and further, toward the horizon.

I ride the range, take a turn in the saddle.

Spend long enough out here and you'll never go back, she prods, and rocking the creaking oiled leather I finger the reins like a string of beads. The sun dips behind the hill, the sky raises her skirts and the periwinkle dusk of her petticoat flirts with deep blue night. We ride in silence, and stars wink into appearance. I feel the deep sigh of the earth settling into sleep, and I know that she's right.

I don't speak, and we stop in the heart of the emptiness. It is big, it is flat, and it is expanding. The wind slips as silk across skin. Dust presses into my clothes, unnamable osmosis, thick in these parts. She is smiling, grin like the moon, beautiful and awful, mysterious and obvious and terrible all at the same time. Silence, a consummate host.

Why did you bring me here, my voice a soft hum in the rush of wind. She shakes out her cigarettes and offers me one. I accept, and she leans in to light it. I smell of her, age, the wisdom of her skin.

Breathing deeply of smoke and air, she looks at the mirror of the moon. Because, she says, voice of honey and certainty. Because every so often, you need to see what you look like

And then,

I am ushered in by nuns and monks, the place where the three-dimensional model of the mandala is displayed. Secretly, I'm glad not be shown to his inner chambers, not sure if I could do all the bowing, the ritual. Fretting about if I brought enough money for my offering, an odd number in an unlabeled envelope. He meets me at the table for my audience, takes my offering graciously, spiritual leader of this institution.

Kind eyes, wrinkled smile. Finding myself spilling, telling him how frustrated I am about the lack of women teachers. He talks about how nuns go to America and don't ever come back, how samsara is open twenty-four seven in America.

But why aren't there any women teachers, I persist, It makes me angry.

Raises eyebrows, genuine concern: Oh no! he says. Don't get angry, don't do that. If you want woman teacher, you become nun and you teach then, he says. He sees the look on my face, and laughs and laughs, joyful.

Good, good, he says. Keep studying, you'll do just fine he says

And then,

Sitting very still, wondering how to say precisely what the hell is going on. That's always the hardest, to clearly say what is actually happening. You can't come at it straight on, really. Reminds me of trying to get inside a painting – if you try to walk right in, head-on, you'll run into the wall like an idiot. I've done that a few times.

But approaching sidelong, being shy about it. Hello there, window, hello world. Sometimes a response comes to the call, a whisper captured, a chirp. A small something, pushing up from the charred body of the world, the remains of who you were, once upon a time. A slender green thing that tickles and muscles its way up through darkness, unfurling through thick mud under hot ash.

This is how, knowing which way to go. A sense of tracking, sharpness in the nose. Bright and active, intuitive, sensing of motion and stillness, emptiness and form. Wanting and wanted, purpose, observations of patterns over time. Longitudinal study of attitudinal behaviors. Artifacts, trinkets, remnants. Not the hero's journey, the queen's path.

Sometimes there are dark unseen things. Sometimes there are bright spots. Very much what it is, whatever it is. Sometimes a sense of regality, supreme delicious secrecy, long procession winding next to the banks of a glorious river, making way in sunlight toward the ocean, washed in fat gold bands of long afternoon sun. Sometimes scratching and clawing, deep dirt under split fingernails teeth grinding sand. Water-logged flesh, frozen shoulders and ropes of hair, the cold wet girl. Tight thin nights of drowning.

Nameless here, though sometimes revealed. Sometimes I let myself be seen. Knowing without words, language the stranger, let me hear you utter. Dear reader, give me your words, urgent now, or maybe slow and sloppy. Breathe them into me, how you call it

And then,

I go for refuge
I pledge allegiance

until I'm enlightened
to the flag

to the Buddha, the Dharma, and the Sangha
of the United States of America

by the merits that I create
and to the Republic

by listening, teaching, and other perfections
for which it stands

may I quickly achieve a state of complete awakening
one nation, under God

for the benefit of all sentient beings
indivisible, with liberty and justice for all

When I listen
I hear formulas

And then,

Walking down the hallway to the bedroom, I catch a glimpse of myself in the mirror. Mirrors are leaks, I read as part of my complete breakfast of champions, and for a few days every mirror I see is leaking all over the place. This hallway, the one with the mirror at the end, is difficult to walk, facing myself the whole way. Arriving in the bedroom, forgetting why I've gone in the first place, how I am going, such a long walk down that hallway. Here is the closet door, unassuming brass knob, closet chamber. In here, maybe? I go in and firmly shut the door.

Shut in the closet, wrapped up in darkness, not touching anything. Proprioception and predisposed knowledge tell me how my body can move in this space. Remembering how my mother experiences claustrophobia, the dream of her shut in her refrigerator. Blind, body and environment, very easy to lose my balance, like standing on one foot with eyes closed. Vestibular balance, I think, and put both my feet on the ground, firm stance. I stretch into intuited periphery, the felt sense of a body in space.

Focusing on breathing, I form the intention to do a simple bow. This is a motion my body knows, can make even in restricted space. Three breaths, and with each exhalation I imagine the space around me expanding out and out, feeling into new boundaries.

Discovering a secret room, the in-betweens, behind the mirror. A large dark hall between daylight spaces. Sweaters stacked, hung mute the sound of elsewhere. My eyes are wide open, staring sightless.

Absent of light, eyes get bored, and brain accommodates with entertainment. Residual bounces, rods and cones, memories of patterns. Remembering how it feels to focus my eyes far away, gazing to a visualized horizon, feeling my muscles responding. My visual cortex, always wanting to please, dances a point of light in my field of vision, asking. Here, is it here, what are you looking for in all this darkness

And then it is there, visualizing something to which I will bow.

Beginning the bow, feeling much taller than I used to be, a long way to the floor in all this darkness. Going down, discovering more than ample time to contemplate the many occasions when the darkness of a closet brought me terror.

Reaching downward, seeking depth, trying not to overreach. Fingertips brush oily carpet. Hands and knees now, breathing deep, flowing. Heart pounding, head cannot find hands triangulated on the floor, I will tip over in this darkness and tumble into the abyss

Flurry panic. Scuffling, a sound from the shoes in the corner, piled invisible, wet stink of leather. I am full of bristling visions of unseen things, breath stopping. Lowering my head further still, finally finding my own hands.

Pouring me out then, all that fear, spilling over, emptying out. A buddha somewhere, dull and dusty, the observer of such offerings, bluntly gold and smiling.

Standing again slowly, carefully. A rush of blood to the head, engorgement that comes with shifting distribution of oxygen, an explosion in the darkness of stars, ghosts of stars, drifting histories. I fold my hands together, dedicate the merits

And then,

I am sitting at my desk, feeling vibrations radiate upward through my feet. The hum causes my keyboard to shiver, tingling fingers. My chair resonates, harmonizing with the relative vibration of objects around me. Water in my glass jiggles, never breaking surface tension. The dog rolls over periodically. The band is rehearsing, musicians practicing art in the basement.

I put on my helmet and dance, right across the page. The effort makes me volatile. Cheeks are flushed, limbs tingle. Dance while you can; dance like you do when no one is watching. Write like no one will see this, not ever. Never. Write like you're the only one who knows this story, because writers must know more than they can afford to know.

Abrupt silence. The music stops and ghosts of pulses dance in the balls of my feet. A soundtrack of creaky ceiling fans and dog sighs. It has been a long day, after all.

For a moment we rest, and when the music begins again I stretch, lungs deep, coughing. Too much smoke and liquor, I chuckle.

Remembering how irony is my favorite kind of joke because irony takes blood. Stretching again, another breath, remembering orange moons reflecting, sun salutations

And then,

I am standing with my feet shoulders' width apart, palms together. Grounded, offering, sweeping my arms up over my head, embracing the sky, inhaling. Palms up, rib cage expanding, inrush of oxygen. Palms come together again over my head. Exhaling then, alerting, moving hands to heart: I am about to move with intention.

Again sweeping arms above head, inhaling. Relaxing downward: fingertips fall into fingers easing into palms which flop into wrists loosening elbows dropping shoulders freeing arms collapsing neck rolling spine down bending knees flopping forward, a rag doll puppet hung on strings of hips. Folded over, emptied out, pouring this offering into the ground.

Inhaling then, new breath lifts me to half-plank, and I try my level best to emulate a t-square. I am that most unnatural figure, somehow the ninety degree angle / *all my limbs are sticks and lines / my head a point upon my spine / can't get no quadrilateral / can't say half empty or half full now*

The sun hits the crown of my head and heat spreads through me, elevated internal temperature, light sweat on clavicles. Fingertips point to ground and then reach toward the earth, seeking. Half-plank, plank. Arms straight, shoulders above wrists. Legs extending behind, head in line with spine, suddenly isosceles. Army style even, the top of a push up, a very hard place to find rest, to hang out, to be at ease.

So almost immediately, bending elbows, lowering to stomach, snake-like. Going slow, slow, it will be so good to rest when I get there, my arms trembling even to support my own weight, elbows tucked close to my body. I can enjoy this challenge because reward is just before me now, just below, waiting.

Stomach on hot wood, peeling underbelly, scratchy sloughing. Forehead to floor, nose in dirt, making an offering of myself, lowest of the low. I am washed with sun, for a moment I rest. And then lift from the top of my head, lift my face to the light. Cobra, rising upward, hood and heart opening. Taking my time, looking around, smiling, elbows and palms alternating for arch and length. Maybe snake, maybe sphinx, maybe lower my head to the ground once more, be all these things. Humble.

Push into palms and knees to be table, push into toes and lift hips to be dog. My head goes down, hips in the air, and my body forms a triangle with the earth. Playful, downward-facing dog, eager and submissive.

Hanging out upside down, ass over teakettle. Struggling to let go, let my head hang down, fighting not to look up and see what is around, such a vulnerable position. Yes, I'll be playful. Oh yes, I'm begging, see me? Come play with me, I'm the downward facing dog. I take a deep breath. My legs hurt. Bring them forward, one lunge and another, crouching. Deep breath. Slight vertigo.

Then standing, in reverse order of descending. First ankles, then knees, then hips. Arms hanging forward, rolling up spine, feeling every inch, each vertebra stacking. Then neck and head, rolling shoulders back once to open chest, heart. A deep breath opens my arms again to the sky, I wave to an airplane passing by, and then vajra palms to heart, hands together with thumbs tucked in.

Filled with the warm red vitality of the sun, shining on my face, backs of eyelids coated with amber. The exercise causes my whole body to awaken, and now I feel motivated to go inside and sit down and write. Suddenly, I can be anywhere: a rooftop in Nepal, a balcony in the city, an old deck in summertime Georgia.

A thunderstorm rumbles in the distance

And then,

I am in my room in Bouda. I have a main room with a bed, a desk, a couch by the window, and a small bookshelf that serves as an altar. An ashtray, a bathroom, a kitchen with a sink and fridge. A western style toilet. Comparatively, I am living in deep luxury, and not a day goes by that I don't give thanks for this flat in the cloister of buildings circling the stupa. The stupa has been here over 1000 years. I have been here less than one.

I am planning to leave for market. Putting on my satchel, adjusting my sweater, unlocking the padlock on the door. Both the door and the metal gate are accordion style, clattering back with a little muscle. Pocketing the lock I draw back the door and gasp: a white dog sits at my door, husky like. It has one blue eye and one brown or green eye, and somehow has made it past the locked gate and guard downstairs.

The dogs in Nepal bark all night long, roam the streets in packs. The guide says carry a big stick, and don't go alone if you're a woman. This dog has landed here, outside my door.

I shut the door. I take a deep breath, close my eyes. Open my eyes. Open the door. The dog is sitting proper, looking at me, quizzical head cock dirty friendly.

I sit down on the floor, separated from the dog by interlaced metal netting. The dog is at ease at my doorway, perky, looking at me. I think, I should take a picture, no one will believe me. Knowing if I move suddenly, if I disengage, if I flash a camera the dog will leave. Hello, I say to the dog.

The dog lies down, looks at me. Its white coat is caked with the red dust and black smoke of outside. Panting. A cut on its face, maybe fighting. Maybe rabies, I think.

You must be hungry, I say to the dog. How did you get in here. Offering my hand just inside the netting, smell of me. Feel of me, what feeling of you.

I start to fret. This dog is hungry, has come here for something. I must feed this dog because I must eat, I need to leave my room to find food for the day. I can not leave to find food until I feed this dog.

Wait just a minute, I say. I go to the kitchen. I have no food that I would think to feed a dog, no dog food. I want to make a good offering. I have only *tsampa*, barley flour, and water. Mixing these together, I bring small morsels to the dog, panting heavily now, maybe injured. Is this the right thing. Will the dog return here again wanting food. Will the guard beat the dog. Will the dog attack me when I go to market.

Feeding, small rolled bits of tsampa, warm licks, snuffled nuzzling. Intimate. Nurturing, looking at this being, soft heart opening. Stray, hungry, alone.

I know this feeling, I say. More than a broken lineage, no lineage at all. The offering is consumed.

Okay, I say. That's what I have, I have to go now, I say. Maybe some water to help with the flour you just ate, I say.

I go to the kitchen and find a bowl, fill it with water, no longer afraid. Returning to the doorway I see a trail of breadcrumbs, the white dog has gone.

I leave the water outside the gate

And then,

I cook a special sauce for myself, spaghetti and garlic bread. Funny how in Nepal, Italian food reminds me of home. Finishing those morsels of comfort, curtains lifting in the wind, veils part and people move in the street below. Thick ropy lines of electrical wire cross the bars on my window and cast shadows. I am alone at the end of the world.

Outside my window, retinues of dakinis amass, weighing heavy on the branches of a tree in the walled garden across the street. I sit on my worn couch and stare through the iron bars, smoking, watching blackbird after blackbird take to the tree.

The branches are heavy with them, cawing and talking to one another. From my room on the second floor I can see beyond the walls of the enclosure. There is a young woman in a purple veil, walking in the garden. She is beautiful and hidden, her shoulders delicate and strong. She is watching the birds also.

My awareness is co-opted then, blackbird dakinis, the dance of why and how. I sit with these birds, feel how they are there for me, and not wanting to know. Remembering, the same feeling as walking onto the back porch and seeing the walls made of sliding glass doors, each one showing a different landscape. Clinging to the threshold of the house, recognizing doors I can't come back from, seasons that cannot be changed. I see these birds and feel this same sensation.

They stay as the sun goes down, I chain smoke and watch. They cackle outside, laughing at me swearing to them that I will translate, communicate from one language to another. They mock me, my green preening, sophomoric optimism. I swear it, and they stay with me, through the visions, cawing. They stay through the writing, through the endless wandering, the longing, the defeat, the destruction, the creation, the generation.

The dakinis hang in the tree as I chase around my room, trying to find the brutal mosquitoes torturing me out of sleep. My intention is to kill them. Mosquitoes in Nepal are huge, relentless. Every time I turn the light on they disappear, but in the darkness they hum in my ears, longing, pleading, whining, aggressive.

Finally, I give up. Come to me, I say. Come take what you need, let it fill you, be full up with me. The birds in the tree outside hush and ruffle feathers as I give myself over, submit to the will of the mosquitoes, make my bed and lie down in it, naked. Vulnerable, exposed. Let them taste of me. Defeated. Embracing lowest of the low, let them have what they want, do what they will.

Bite me, I say, and stay present with every damn one, feel what is taken and what is created. What cost of experience, sharing, lessening self. Exhaustion takes me and I drift into shifting dream sleep, green tara ushering, in the morning the birds are gone

And then,

It is Tuesday night when the thing in my chest finally moves. It has been sitting here for days, a tight aching knot of something that makes me feel like crying, keeps me from even thinking about next steps. It climbs into my throat and sticks in my craw, my mouth opening and closing and nothing comes out. I finally get a breath and my head is pounding, reverberating, and it drops back into my chest, the worst heartache I've ever felt. I rock myself back and forth, sobbing, as it climbs and sinks, climbs and sinks.

Finally I have hold of it, locked in my throat. Holding my attention there, massaging it gently, squeezing and releasing. What is it, what is it, I keep asking myself. What is this.

A word comes floating up from the thick ache: sadness. Breathing, keeping my attention even, not taking or leaving. Sadness, I say to myself, and with a gelatinous pop it comes into my head. Pain, oh pain, oh throbbing pain ricochet in my skull. Still the attention, the light attention, gently feeling the edges. What is it, I say. What is this. Who are you.

Again a word comes up from it, spreading into my left cheekbone, behind my right eye. Guilt, it says, throbbing alive, a wash of pain through my sinuses, reaching up into my cranium. Dissipating.

And then a hard, hurtful nugget, a thick little plug of pain remains. Refusing to move, refusing to be anywhere, I hold my attention with it, breathing. This little plug of thick rubber pain stuck in my skull, on the right side, just above my eye.

Exhaustion threatens to overcome me, the storm sufficiently quieting. I stay, unthinking attention, squeezing and releasing this knot. It goes slow, so slow, up the inside curve of my skull, above my right eye. Stuck, this pain, dense and magnetic, the whole way. I stay and stay, What is it, I say. What is it, what are you small one the smallest densest thickest slowest most hidden one what is it what is it

Crumbling, softening. Hurt.

Hurt, I say, and throb gently. Yes, just simple. Plain on its face, hurt.

Old young hurt softened. It doesn't dissipate upward, out of the top of my head, as I thought might happen. Don't make me go. Don't make me leave or push me away. Just stay. Hold. And softening, this hurt. Melting, dripping, dissolving through my bone structure, dripping down the back of my throat. I have had echoes of it since, but nothing quite as strong

And then,

I am looking out my office window, springtime. Fat bees weave and bob around the flowering branches of the tree, I am watching the breeze and the sunlight and the mellow buzz.

A little bird lands on a flowering branch, cherry blossom, wind-up chirping. Its wings are tipped with purple. It cocks its head, bright black eye, opens its beak and says to me

Somebody is dreaming the war into being.

I flutter, is it me. I'm sorry, I say. I don't know my own power. Why didn't you tell me.

The bird ruffles its feathers, weaves among bees, head bobbing. Eyeballs a plump one for snacking, bristling legs broken, wings in beak.

We had forgotten, the bird says, swallowing hard. It is a disease, this war. Internal battles wage. You aim for peaceful gain, gaining peace, but what embrace will satisfy the child who will not kill.

What embrace indeed, I say, and then the bird is off, winging through the sunlight, the drone of bees

And then,

I look down and see faded purple socks, like my sister used to have. They are sticking out from beneath the closet door. This image drives me to night terror, the dread realization that the other mother is in there, listening. The wrongness of it, those feet pigeon toed out from the lip of the door, my stomach suddenly stuck in my throat, cheeks flushed. She is listening, she heard me, the hardwood floor, the thick, pitted paint on the doorframe, feeling echoes of terror bouncing round in my chest.

In the dream, I am living the narrative of a young woman, maybe late teens, maybe older than her years. I have dark, straight hair, worn to my shoulder, bangs cut straight across. Unkempt, a page boy, a servant of sorts. I am standing at the bathroom mirror, and have just finished cleaning the flat. She will be home soon, I have a few minutes to myself, I'm going to smoke out the bathroom window. These are the rules: I can live here as long as she never sees me, hears me, sees evidence of my existence. I have to keep everything clean.

The bathroom is small, a long closet in grey green blue tiles. At the far end of the room is an old cast-iron affair, claw foot tub. High on the wall above is a small sliding glass window, patterned with opaque glass. I climb up on the lip of the tub and slide it open. It is dirty, but I can prop my elbows on the sill and still make a light.

I keep my face up near the window, leaning to blow the smoke outside. I can feel the fresh air on my face and close my eyes for a moment, thinking bitter, water stained thoughts. The story starts here, paranoia about her smelling the smoke, vast anxiety, self deprecating and cynical voice. Embittered, somehow enslaved, fear and love and guilt.

Sliding the window shut, stepping off the edge of the tub. I am silent over the creaking hardwood floorboards, I know where every step is to move silently, unnoticed across the living room. White ceiling and walls, built-in bookshelves, books everywhere, I've never been anywhere outside this inside. Hardbacks, paperbacks, backpacks, stacks and stacks.

Socks sliding silently past comfortable ratty old furniture. Dust free, everything just so in eccentric order, old doilies spiderwebbing across end tables holding lacy tasseled lampshades. I have to keep everything just so, nothing out of place, or she will rage her terrible rage, she will have to remind me, teach me of the rules yet another time

Dead stop. Suddenly, center of the floor, heart thudding, I see a woman in the living room. Thought I was home alone, but there is a woman in this room with me. She is sitting in the corner, awkward. She is in a stuffed chair of mottled gold, eyes wide and silent. She sees me, I see her and I take a deep breath and then

You have to help me, she says.

Must be a guest of the other mother, I think. This woman from outside somewhere, from somewhere else, some other neck of the woods.

Can't help you, I'm not here, I say. I know better than to interfere, just stick to the routine, follow the formula and cover my tracks. She doesn't even want to know I'm here, you know. I'm really surprised you can even see me. I start walking again, my silent slipper whisper through the room.

I can help you if you help me, she says. I know what's happening, it doesn't have to happen this way, she says. But you have to help me. I stare at her. Slowly, she rotates her arms above her head, revealing them from behind the chair. Impossible, around the world contortion. Her wrists are handcuffed together, she is showing them to me and calm is struggling to stay on her face.

Her showing me these handcuffs is risky. If the other mother put her in handcuffs, she's in deep. By showing me these handcuffs, she isn't playing along, she isn't following the rules. Better if you just do what you are told, don't risk the retribution. I nod when I see her handcuffs. Whatever she'd done, it was bad. She was going to get it.

I'm taking a risk even talking to you, I say. I'm pretty sure I'm a prisoner here too, and you'll learn, she has her way of punishing. You're in for it now, I say, and because I know that lesson I quote it to her.

Reciting it from one of the books on the shelf, a book I helped to write, a book I had written. I know exactly where that book lives, what shelf, in what order. Reciting, I can hear my voice, hear her voice in my voice. Can see the words on the page.

The passage echoes with volume, the locks on all the rooms tumbling at once, hammers falling in my head staggering, I am staggering. The book I just quoted in my own voice. Maybe not the other mother living here, maybe I wrote that passage quoted to the prisoner. It was me: I wrote that. Vertigo, the room upends, sitting down hard on my ass.

Help is on the way, the woman in the chair says, and I am wondering out loud if I am somehow the trouble, was she here to see me or the other woman, was she here to see me? Lock me up further, take me away? Did I, was I the one who put her in

And then suddenly, painfully, the narrative collapses. I am the author. I am the other mother, and somehow also the woman sitting in the chair, I am the monster who handcuffed this poor woman to the chair, god I bet she's some kind of therapist or literary critic, you just watch. I don't remember her, or maybe I had lunch with her, I don't feel like I've ever seen her before, but maybe she was there all along, just like me.

It is okay, she is nodding. There are others flooding in now, official types, uniforms and badges and pulsing lights. She is free and explaining to a cop and I am feeling a little unsteady on my pins, standing in the hallway. She comes over to talk to me, she touches my arm reassuringly.

Telling her things, about how it was imprisoned, explaining how it was to her when I notice: two feet, clad in purple socks, sticking out from underneath the door of the hallway closet. The closet next to the shelf with that book, never seen a door there before.

I stop speaking, mid sentence, horror. She has heard everything I've said to this woman, and there will be a lofty bill to pay. I am frozen by fear. The woman holding me, touching my arms, seeing the horror on my face, the dread of my body. She follows my gaze and sees me staring at those feet, those purple socks sticking out from the closet.

You are seeing something, she says. There is something in that closet that you see. Her protector friends draw near, sensing.

My eyes are fixed. I push a trembling finger to my lips. Shhhhhhh, I whisper.

She approaches the door with one hand firmly grasping my forearm. She opens the door with the faded purple socks sticking out and the other mother is there, the face of her revealed.

Her eyes stare sightlessly, sweatered arms clenched tightly like flightless wings. Her stiff body, stuffed in among the coats, tumbles forward. Terror; I thought she was under the floorboards, she caught me in a conversation about how things really are

And her lifeless form falls into my arms, taking her weight into me.

I am so gentle with her, so full of love for her, even as she hurt me. I am cradling her head to me and smelling her hair, I am weeping. I am lowering her to the ground, kindling, we slowly descend together

And then,

I am a demoness. I am huge, many stories high, and my body is black with white markings on it, stripes like a tiger, but not as regular. My face is white but I have deep rings of black around my eyes, black hair, black mouth. I am naked and ferocious, bone ornaments swinging.

Fierce, but not nearly as demonic as my male counterpart. He is huge, horns, long fangs, wild rolling eyes. He has captured me here, is taking great delight in terrifying me. We are in the middle of the road on a gray desert plane, and there might be some single standing trees, leafless branches twisting in the distance. The sky is dark and full of fire and stars. He is coming after me from down this road, and I am lying prone, nowhere to go. I watch him coming. He is going to rape me, I think. He wants me frightened.

And I am frightened, but there is no where to run any more. As he draws near I lie on the earth and open my arms and legs, my self to him. He mutters curses at me, threats, about how he can hurt me, can grow as long as he wants he will rip right through me. I lay my head on the earth and take him in, reach behind him with my hands. I grab fistfuls of knotted hair and pull down to me, whispering through demoness teeth chiding

You fool No matter how big you are how long how terrible I am deeper You are with me under my stars I swallow you whole I keep entire universes in my womb

Speaking, feeling the power come out of him, taking it all everything inside me, all he can give, more. Depth in my body opens infinitely, a deep well of accommodation his aggression can not fathom. I wake immediately

And then,

I know you in that forest then, the interlacing of branches.
Seeing the pattern of you there, what falls before me, moving
along the ground. Subversive, looking for the roots of roots,
gone to seed. There appears an inclination toward art. There
appears a need for connection with that which comes through
unconventional means, what comes up from below, lotus-like.
Listening and repeating, call and response.

Wise of me not to move, to be still in this just now. These
skandhas, heaps that make up this self of existence. Cumulative,
exclusive, transcendent all. Elevating aspect and attribute, form
is emptiness and emptiness is form. Let me repeat, how love calls
you by your name.

Art making, love making, form making. Form in relationship
with emptiness, shape and space, frame and framed, challenged
by the distance between extremes, center and periphery,
the center does not hold. Desire, the agency of bliss, union.
Choosing limits, defining boundaries.

Imagining the moment I am born. My mother's pain is bright,
my own bewilderment suddenly clouds amniotic clarity. Cold
sharp air against wet skin for the first time, suddenly aware of
outside, knowing such a thing as outside exists. The beginning of
other, self and mother, the beginning of self having so separated.
Stark. No choice but to go forward, outward, onward.

Imagining the moment of my death. Death comes to take me in,
work me back into the fold. I feel how it comes, no choice but
to go on and leave this behind. I perceive a moment of this, this
lifetime, right now.

Just for a moment, there is a sense of what comes before and after, and I can see now clearly. This fulcrum where the balance swings weightless.

In this moment, it is not so impossible to believe that there is love so passionate, desire so driven that it joyfully creates.

Who wouldn't choose such a thing, if they were offered, I wonder. No answer to my question comes and so I move again, leafy underbelly.

Silence responds in disarming chansons, breezing through the trees.

And then,

I am sitting with my mother, holding hands. She has just told me the story of my conception, the darkness in which I was conceived, the intimate vulnerability.

I've never told that to anyone before, she says, blushing. I see the girl in her, and I tell her I will keep her secret, blushing myself. I get a glimpse of how they are in me, mother and father.

We talk deep into the night, late-night talk-shows come and go, dull glow from the muted television. We share stories, memories, laughing together. Eventually, sleep begins to overtake us. As all things do, we come around to death, and she is describing to me her wishes for her body *post mortem*.

Deep breath, stinging tears, prickle glass eyes. Looking at her face, seeing her gaze, watching her as she scans that unseen horizon.

I will be there, I say. I can help you. I will help you find your next rebirth. Offering. She is holding my hand, touching my face, wiping away my tears.

Oh kiddo, she whispers. You promise?

I love you, I say

And then,

I am dedicating the merits.

May I quickly achieve a state of complete awakening for the benefit of all sentient beings.

May all sentient beings everywhere realize awakening, even if just for one instant.

May the tender heart of compassion be opened in them, even if just for one moment.

May the suffering of all realms be alleviated, even if just for the span of one breath.

SOURCE MATERIAL
Ordered by time of initial writing

WARRIOR STANCE *october 2001*
MEAT GRINDER *november 2001, dream*
STARS *december 2001, dream*

DEMONESS *february 2002, dream*
WHITE DOG *april 2002*
DAKINIS *april 2002*
YOU TEACH THEN *april 2002*
COWGIRL *may 2002*

CANNOT AFFORD THESE ARTIFACTS *november 2007, dream*
MY STORY FOR YOU *december 2007*
REFUGE *december 2007*

WOODS *may 2008*
STONE SETTING *may 2008*
BEACH LADY *may 2008*
DIRE WOLF *october 2008*
YELLOW SUBMARINE *september 2008, dream*
DALAI LAMA SAYS SPROUT *september 2008*
GENERAL STORE *september 2008, dream*
TUESDAY *september 2008*
RED DOOR IN THE SOUTH *october 2008, dream*
SUN SALUTATION *november 2008*
APPLE POMEGRANATE LOTUS *december 2008, dream*
THE BED IN WHICH I AM CONCEIVED TWO *december 2008*

VICTORIAN HOUSE VIOLINS *january 2009, dream*
ON THE BUS *january 2009*
THE QUEEN'S PATH *march 2009*
THE OTHER MOTHER *april 2009, dream*
ARTMAKING *may 2009*
MODELING ONE *may 2009*
MODELING TWO *may 2009*
PHOTOGRAPH *july 2009*
THE BED IN WHICH I AM CONCEIVED ONE *august 2009, dream*
WAYS UNFED *paragraph 1 & 2: september 2009, paragraph 3: september 2007*
GINGERBREAD *september 2009*
PLUNGE *september 2009*
LINE DRAWING *september 2009*
RABBIT *september 2009*
FLOORBOARDS *september 2009*
APOLOGIST *september 2009*
TREEGARDEN *september 2009, dream*
PERIPHERAL VISION *september 2009*
FRAMES *october 2009*
FORMULAE *october 2009*
CHAMBER MUSIC *october 2009*
REHEARSAL *october 2009*
WIND UP *october 2009*
DEDICATING THE MERITS *october 2009*

ENDNOTES

BETTER NOT TO BEGIN

BEGIN. "It remains to explain that the term *citta* has connotations which are not shared with the standard English translation, 'mind'. There is some sense of active mental process involved in this term, which under some circumstances would mean that *citta* would be better translated as 'thought, attitude' or even 'will', in the sense of 'the will to Awakening'. As it is, 'Awakening Mind' risks the possibility of reification by the unwary reader, and so we hope that readers will remember that the arising of the Awakening Mind involves the internal transformation of the individual rather than the evocation of an external entity." *Bodhicaryavatara (commentary)* [1]

APPLE POMEGRANATE LOTUS

THIS YOUNG SELF. "There are many ways to encounter that child isolated within the self. Often this child appears in dream, sometimes in a drawing or doodle; occasionally she is there in the way a woman dresses or one day, suddenly, wears her hair in braids.But the advent of this child cannot fulfill its promise until she is translated from the symbolic to the emotional sphere . . . if we can tolerate this child she will tell us why we have isolated her from participation in our lives, losing with her the roots of female being." Kim Chernin, *Reinventing Eve* [2]

POMEGRANATES. "Pleasure is a sensation. It is written into our bodies; it is our experience of delight, of joy . . . this knowing becomes a taproot, anchoring the psyche in the body, in relationship, in language and culture." The journey of "coming into consciousness is not simply the replacement of innocence and ignorance with knowingness and selfness. It is also the coming out of dissociation . . . In dissociation, we literally don't know what we don't know; and the process of recovery centers on recovery of voice and with it, the ability to tell one's story." Carol Gilligan, *The Birth of Pleasure* [3]

LOTUS. In the Tibetan tradition, lotuses appear in one of the most popular common mantras, *om mani padme hum* (the jewel is in the lotus). While this refers to the joining of wisdom and method in practice, lotuses are also a metaphor for the female sex, and this mantra has been understood by some as an homage and invocation of the power of female sexuality, the "pearl in the lotus," or clitoris. [4]

WOODS

BELIEVING IMPOSSIBLE THINGS. *Through the Looking Glass And What Alice Found There*, by Lewis Carroll.

CUTTING YOUR TONGUE OUT. Dream, summer teaching, at Deer Park Buddhist Center in Madison, Wisconsin, 2001.

HUT TO HUT. Dream, sometime between ten and twelve years of age.

PURPLE DINNER PLATE. Dream, spring 1999.

THE BED IN WHICH I AM CONCEIVED ONE

I AM SLEEPING. Visiting my sister in her home for the first time. Her guest bedroom houses the bed frame that belonged to my parents during the first years of their marriage.

NO FLYING IN THE HOUSE / MINIATURE TOY DOGS. A book that I read and subsequently stole from my fourth grade classroom, age eight or nine. [5]

FIVE LEGS. "Five Legs," *Wooden Smoke*, Mike Keneally, 2001.

DIRE WOLF

DIRE WOLF. "Dire Wolf," *Reckoning*, Greatful Dead, 1981.

PLUNGE

AVATARA. "The first, *bodhi*, means 'Awakening', while the second, *caryā*, means 'the way to go or act', with metaphorical usages deriving from the sense of the 'proper way', such as 'path', 'good conduct', 'way of life', or 'training'. The final element, *āvatāra*, means literally '(bringing about) a descent into' something, but with the metaphorical usage of 'entrance into', 'introduction to', or 'undertaking'." *Bodhicaryāvatāra (commentary)* [6]

GONE BEYOND. *Prajñāpāramitā* (perfection of wisdom) sutras, specifically the Heart Sutra, the mantra *tayathā gate gate pāragate pārasamgate bodhi svāhā* (gone gone gone beyond utterly gone beyond enlightenment). [7]

RABBIT

I AM A RABBIT. "Backtracking and looping are terms that describe an animal diving underground to escape, and then popping up behind the predator's back . . . Analysis, dream interpretation, self-knowing, exploration, are all undertaken because they are ways of backtracking and looping. They are ways of coming up behind the issue and seeing it from a different perspective." Clarissa Pinkola-Estes, *Women Who Run With the Wolves* [8]

FLOORBOARDS

WRATHFUL EMANATIONS. Vajrayogini[9] is one terrifying woman: her bright red body is vibrant in the sun, the sweat, the dust. She dances furiously, joyously on the corpse of the ignorant mind, the egoistic self. Around her hips and ankles are strings of pearls and bones that swish and snap as she sways her hips, shakes her money-maker. Her red belly has never born children, but she's known the slick of sex. Her hair flies wildly about her, adorned with a crown of skulls and fire. Her lips are curled around sharp, pointed teeth, red lipstick running, death mask grin.

In the crook of her arm she holds a staff, her male principle, her sun king, the fear of death decapitated three times and impaled on a staff bearing the ornamented feathers of her inner flame. She carries a knife of cutting wisdom. In her other hand, she cradles a skull cup of the elixir of life, ambrosia, blood, the water of the fountain, the stuff of dreams, the two-in-one, the wine. Her name is Vajra, the diamond, the adamantine, the lightning, the merciless, the clear, the compassionate, the precise, Yogini, the woman, the sky dancer, the veiled one, the star and night sky herself, the she. Vajrayogini. She is teaching me about embodying the qualities I wish to possess, teaching me how to get up and dance.

"In dream, the karmic traces manifest in consciousness unfettered by the rational mind with which we so often rationalize away a feeling or a fleeting mental image ... the dynamics are easier to understand in dream, because they can be observed free of the limitations of the physical world and the rational consciousness." Tenzin Wangyal, *The Tibetan Yogas of Dream and Sleep* [10]

UNDER THE FLOORBOARDS. "The Castle is outwardly dedicated to lofty abstractions, the pursuit of the Arts and Sciences, and is only able to achieve this through an unbalanced, one-sided development of the forces of the human soul; it needs to deny and hide away under lock and key the primal Venus forces in the soul, the powerful passions of the feminine side of human nature. Because of this distorted polarization – this fear of the masculine powers in the realm of the Castle of being engulfed by the powerful feminine energies – any meeting between the masculine and feminine must result in inner struggle and death." *The Chemical Wedding of Christian Rosenkreutz* (commentary) [11]

VICTORIAN VIOLINS

VICTORIAN HOUSES. "If I were asked to name the chief benefit of the house, I should say: The house shelters the day-dreaming, the house protects the dreamer, the house allows one to dream in peace ... the cellar dreamer knows that the walls of the cellar are buried walls, walls that have the entire earth behind them... buried madness, walled-in tragedy." Gaston Bachelard, *The Poetics of Space* [12]

WAYS UNFED

RE-ENTRANT LOOPS, RECIPROCAL NETS. "It is helpful to be able to imagine the development of the neocortex in the individual for this reason: if it is traced from the beginning, and if it is understood without dualist metaphor, it is apparent that the development of the neocortex proceeds in contact with the rest of the nervous system, that the development of the nervous system proceeds in contact with the rest of the organism, and that the development of the organism proceeds in contact with local parts of the larger world." Susan Oyama, *The Problem of Change* [13, 13-1]

WAYS UNFED. Ellie Epp, September 2007.

YELLOW SUBMARINE

GONE, GOING HOME. "The Boxer," *Bridge Over Troubled Water*, Simon and Garfunkel, 1968.

PHOTOGRAPH

LINEAGE. "If we listen well to the connotations of 'irrational' they are highly charged: we hear overtones of 'hysteria' (that disease once supposed to arise in the womb) . . . the term 'rational' relegates to its opposite term all that it refuses to deal with, and thus ends by assuming itself to be purified of the nonrational, rather than searching to identify and assimilate its own surreal or nonlinear elements. This single error may have mutilated patriarchal thinking – especially scientific and philosophic thinking – more than we yet understand." Adrienne Rich, *Of Woman Born* [14]

A can of worms, indeed: apples everywhere shot through with rot. Remembering who came before, because that's part of this, too. An apple crammed into the mouth of a pig, glazed in honey and sugar, glistening fat and plump, splitting skin spitting over fire. Stoke the coals, a long slow burn.

"Womenfolk are uncontrolled, Ananda. Womenfolk are envious, Ananda. Womenfolk are greedy, Ananda. Womenfolk are weak in wisdom, Ananda. She will even when going along stop to ensnare the heart of a man: whether standing, sitting, or lying down, laughing, talking, or singing, weeping, stricken or dying, a woman will stop to ensnare the heart of a man."[15]

And yet Padmasambhava, addressing his consort and human manifestation of the Queen of Dakinis says, "The basis for realizing enlightenment is a human body. Male or female – there is no great difference. But if she develops the mind bent on enlightenment, the woman's body is better." [16]

"The tragedy here is that though Buddhists have all the analytical tools needed to deconstruct a conventional ego, including its gendered dimensions, traditional Buddhism has put all of its energy into deconstructing ego while leaving gender largely intact." Rita Gross, *A Garland of Feminist Reflections* [17]

However, "when the *yab-yum* (father-mother) iconography is analyzed only politically, as an expression of male and female power, most of its significance is lost. The central point of the practice is to give up the usual habit of subjectifying or objectifying gender or any other concepts of self and other, and to realize the interdependent play of phenomena as expressions of the natural state." Judith Simmer-Brown, *Dakini's Warm Breath* [18]

IMPLYING A FUTURE. I would've been the first among them to burn. How I dare to learn philosophies, religions, the sciences. Terrorism in raw form. I would have been dragged by my unbounded hair, jailed and raped and tortured, carved out with sharp pieces of stone and shell, or maybe a coat hanger. I would have been tied high above the fire so that I would burn slowly, so that I could feel the pain of my bubbling flesh and illuminated screaming, suffering well for my transgressions.

My scientist heroes did not defend me then, any more than they do now. Studying them today makes me quaint, cute, kind of geeky for a girl. Had I been a contemporary and tried to share their science, I would have been silenced. 1750: I burned at the stake. 1850: I was cured of my hysteria with the first successful hysterectomy. 1950: I drifted silently on Valium. [19]

"(kill the woman who studies history the repetition is so obvious this redundancy 200 million sperm per shot repeat repeat) & she abides it again & again abets it as if *the human condition* & every wound becomes a religion becomes a prison becomes an industry that makes new wounds bigger nastier more profitable repeat repeat &my sex colludes w/this desecration of (our)Nature until it becomes Our Nature" Susan Griffin, *Woman and Nature* [20]

MODELING ONE

MY MIND WANDERS. "Nothing happens: it is absolutely boring... traveling the path means you get off everything; there is no place to perch. Sit and feel your breath, be with it... even your watcher is unsympathetic to you, begins to mock you. Boredom is important because boredom is anticredential . . . it increases the psychological sophistication of the practitioners." Chogyam Trungpa, *The Essential Chogyam Trungpa* [21]

ON THE BUS

TINY DANCER. "Tiny Dancer," *Madman Across the Water*, Elton John, 1971.

MODELING TWO

TO OTHERS I SEEM DULL AND SLOW. "Others have more than they need, but I alone have nothing. I am a fool. Oh, yes! I am confused. Others are clear and bright, but I alone am dim and weak. Others are sharp and clever, but I alone am dull and stupid. Oh, I drift like the waves of the sea, without direction, like the restless wind. Everyone else is busy, but I alone am aimless and depressed. I am different. I am nourished by the great mother." Lao Tzu, *Tao Te Ching* [22]

STARS

MERCURY AND MADNESS. In three dimensions, gravity has a certain appeal, a certain gravitas / a means of orienting / a special kind of immutable quality / that appeals to reason. It makes sense, in the sense that most of the time / it does not surprise.

An apple falls from a tree and formulates a legend / a story that can be told / and re-told / with relative certainty, never mind that Newton was a mad man. A mercurial fanatic. Revelation requires such uncompromising extremes.

I am on an airplane, and the airplane has no agency. An extension of inertia, falling through space / and I wonder about bodies in motion / and the illusion of control. Journal, 9.24.09

ONE WHITE SNAKE. "Before the Queen stood an altar, small but exquisitely decorated, on which were a black velvet book discreetly overlaid with gold, and beside it a small taper in an ivory candlestick. For all its smallness it burned on and on, and if Cupid had not sometimes blown on it for fun, we would not have taken it for a fire. Near this stood a sphere or celestial globe, turning neatly on its own; also a little striking clock; and next a tiny crystal fountain out of which a clear blood-red liquid continually ran; and lastly a skull in which was a white snake, so long that although it crawled round and encircled all the objects, its tail remained in one of the eyeholes of the skull until its head came back to the other, so that it never left its skull." *The Chemical Wedding of Christian Rosenkreutz* [23]

COWGIRL

WOODPECKER KIND OF TUNE. See *Still Life With Woodpecker*, Tom Robbins.

NO SHAPE, NO COLOR. "Shariputra, a son or daughter of the lineage who wishes to engage in the practice of the profound perfection of wisdom should view it like this: he or she should correctly see the five aggregates, and see that they are empty of inherent existence. Form is empty; emptiness is form. Emptiness is not separate from form, and form is not separate from emptiness . . . therefore, Shariputra, in emptiness there is no form, no feeling, no conception, no compositional factors, no consciousness. There is no eye, no ear, no nose, no tongue, no body, no mind; no form, no sound, no smell, no taste, no tactile object, no phenomena. . . likewise, there is no suffering, origin, cessation, or path; no gnosis, no attainment, and also no non-attainment." *The Heart of the Venerable Mother Prajnaparamita: The Perfection of Wisdom* [24]

THE QUEEN'S PATH

HELLO WORLD. "Hello world" is a common first exercise for learning computer programming languages.

CHARRED BODY OF THE WORLD. Vajrayogini / Chakrasamvara texts arise from the "'cult of the charnel ground', consisting of antinomian yogins, yoginis, and various renunciants who chose a deliberately transgressive lifestyle, drawing their garb and, in part, sustenance from the liminal space of the charnel ground that was the locus for their meditative and ritual activities." David B. Gray, *The Cakrasamvara Tantra* [25]

TIGHT THIN NIGHTS. "Look at that woman, once the ecstatic child, who walks slowly but undeniably further and further into her remoteness. Not so lonely – not so lonely there, really . . . the world flat and drained of color – only shades of gray and then and then . . . but the world was losing its vibrancy, its color, its feeling. She felt herself in a shroud of white. And how the snow seemed muffled. The snow – not possible to move through anymore. And the cold." Carole Maso, *Break Every Rule* [26]

"Women speak: they describe a time when they 'felt frozen,' 'like stone,' when they were 'buried in sand.' Some feel 'inwardly dead'. Many women are familiar with this struggle; few name it correctly or associate it with an underlying quest to create a self." Kim Chernin, *Reinventing Eve* [27]

CHAMBER MUSIC

MIRRORS ARE LEAKS. See *Breakfast of Champions*, Kurt Vonnegut.

THE FELT SENSE OF A BODY IN SPACE. "Through a special mapping procedure, your brain annexes space to your limbs and body, clothing you in it like an extended, ghostly skin. The maps that encode your physical body are connected directly, immediately, personally to a map of every point in that space and also a map of your potential to perform actions in that space. Your self does not end where your flesh ends, but suffuses and blends with the world, including other beings." Sandra & Matthew Blakeslee, *The Body Has a Mind of Its Own* [28]

A SIMPLE BOW. Standing with feet shoulder width apart, bringing palms together, thumbs tucked in. Lifting hands over the crown of the head, bringing them down again to forehead, symbolizing body. Then lower, to the level of throat, symbolizing speech. Finally, returning to the center of the chest, symbolizing mind, the three being the offering made with the bow. Continuing the descent, folding the body over, rolling downward, palms finding the floor. Finding ways to hands and knees, pouring self out the top of head, exhaling. Inhaling again, pushing up to hands and knees, then again to standing, bringing arms up and palms again together, above the crown to begin another bow. Traditionally, this bow is repeated three times.

REHEARSAL

PUT ON MY HELMET AND DANCE. "Embodied writing brings the finely textured experience of the body to the art of writing . . . as a style of writing, embodied writing is itself an act of embodiment. Writers attune to the movements of water, earth, air, and fire, whichever coax our bodily sense to explore. Continuing to write in a Cartesian style seems no longer acceptable, especially in the fields of transpersonal psychology, consciousness studies, health psychology, and positive psychology. Disembodied writing just perpetuates the subject-object bifurcation between the world of our bodies and the world we inhabit." Rosemarie Anderson, *Embodied Writing & Reflections on Embodiment* [29]

SUN SALUTATION

PALMS TOGETHER. Yoga is "the joining of the mind to a natural, pristine, actual meaning. This is mainly the un-differentiable joining of method and wisdom, which is identified as the un-differentiable joining of the mind of enlightenment and the perfection of wisdom realizing emptiness." Tenzin Gyatso, H.H. XIV Dalai Lama, *Yoga Tantra* [30]

HALF FULL NOW. "Where Have You Gone," *Skittish*, Mike Doughty, 2004.

INRUSH OF OXYGEN. "Tantra is that body of beliefs and practices which, working from the principle that the universe we experience is nothing other than the concrete manifestation of the divine energy of the godhead that creates and maintains that universe, seeks to ritually appropriate and channel that energy, within the human microcosm, in creative and emancipatory ways." David Gordon White, *Tantra In Practice* [31]

TUESDAY

THE THING IN MY CHEST FINALLY MOVES. See *Focusing*, Eugene Gendlin.

WIND-UP

WHAT EMBRACE. Stay / stay a little longer /
timid shadow / of my repose /
fastened so lightly / to the breath before /
my first question /
Thou art the hunger / can disarm / every appetite /
What embrace / satisfies the child /
who will not kill?

"Stay," *The Energy of Slaves*, Leonard Cohen, 1972.

DEMONESS

UNDER MY STARS. "Every man and every woman is a star. O azure-lidded woman, bend upon them! I am known to ye by my name Nuit, and to him by a secret name which I will give him when at last he knoweth me . . . And the sign shall be my ecstasy, the consciousness of the continuity of existence, the omnipresence of my body . . .Invoke me under my stars! Love is the law, love under will. Nor let the fools mistake love; for there are love and love. There is the dove, and there is the serpent. Choose ye well! I am the blue-lidded daughter of Sunset; I am the naked brilliance of the voluptuous night-sky. To me! To me!" Aleister Crowley, *Liber AL vel Legis* [33]

ARTMAKING

GONE TO SEED. "Our understanding of what the mind is matters deeply. Our most basic philosophical beliefs are tied inextricably to our view of reason. Reason has been taken for over two milennia as the defining characteristic of human beings. Reason includes not only our capacity for logical inference, but also our ability to conduct inquiry, to solve problems, to evaluate, to criticize, to deliberate about how we should act, and to reach an understanding of ourselves, other people, and the world. A radical change in our understanding of reason is therefore a radical change in our understanding of ourselves." George Lakoff & Mark Johnson, *Philosophy in the Flesh: The Embodied Mind and its Challenge to Western Thought* [34]

"Masculine intellectual systems are inadequate because they lack the wholeness that female consciousness, excluded from them, could provide. Truly to liberate women, then, means to change thinking itself: to reintegrate what has been named the unconscious, the subjective, the emotional within the structural, the rational, the intellectual . . . and finally to annihilate those dichotomies." Adrienne Rich, *Of Woman Born* [35]

"So deep is our modern disembodiment that many of us have no trust in the body whatsoever and content ourselves with disregarding it on every occasion and at every possible level. In all of this, not suprisingly, there is rarely any sense that the body, on its own and from its own side, might have something to offer us; that the body might, in some sense, be more intelligent than our conscious self or ego; that the body might have its own designs from which - if understood - we might stand to benefit a very great deal." Reginald Ray, *Touching Enlightenment: Finding Realization in the Body* [36]

"If any problem qualifies as the problem of consciousness, it is this one. Even when we have explained the performance of all the cognitive and behavioral functions in the vicinity of experience - perceptional discrimination, categorization, internal access, verbal report - there may still remain a further unanswered questions: Why is the performance of these functions accompanied by experience? Why doesn't all this information-processing go on 'in the dark,' free of any inner feel?" David Chalmers, *Philosophy of Mind, Classical and Contemporary Readings* [37]

"Thus a pressing question for our modern world is: does a way exist to integrate the power of religion and of science for the physical, mental, and spiritual well-being of humanity? We are faced with the challenge of restoring our own subjectivity to the natural world, acknowledging its meaningful role in nature." B. Alan Wallace, *The Taboo of Subjectivity: Toward a New Science of Consciousness* [38]

"Studying consciousness will change your life. At least if you study it deeply and thoroughly, it will . . . none of us can thoroughly expect to 'understand consciousness'. I am not even sure what that would mean. Nonetheless I do know that when people really struggle with the topic, they find that their own experience and their own sense of self change in the process. Happily, most of the changes are, in the end, positive and the students are glad to have been through them. Even so, I can only repeat my warning and hope you will take it seriously." Susan Blackmore, *Consciousness: An Introduction* [39]

BY YOUR NAME. "Love Calls You By Your Name," *Songs of Love and Hate*, Leonard Cohen, 1970.

And then,

I am standing in a hall full of righteous anger, archways of established power. Engulfed by my own certainty, my fingers are snaked in the short purple curls of a woman kneeling before me. She is screaming, and I stand clutching the nape of her neck, forcing her gaze across the threshold. I want her to see it, I am making her look at it, I am screaming at her to look at it, asserting my will that she see.

A teacher appears suddenly, speaking sharply. As she speaks, false walls are revealed in the structure, carved tunnels choked with hidden rooms appearing. The carnal ruse of conspiracy, revealing relationships, context, dynamic hierarchy shaping my actions.

Immediately I am humbled by my own ambitions. Embarrassed by my own enlargement, my own gross inflations, fingers that clutch and then relax. Seeing how I affirm and undermine the risk, the entire undertaking, exacting balances. My role in the *lila*, this play.

Looking at her, knowing how you must pay with your own death

and remembering my mother saying to me,
what doesn't kill you makes you stronger.

What doesn't kill you? I think

and I feel the tide rising again,
the aching battle cry

an impassioned plea
to other daughters like me

don't give up

And then,

I am standing in the formal living room with my sister, just before dawn. We are in baggy t-shirts and socks, whispering in the still sleeping house.

Two large windows overlook the front yard, where a stand of old trees (the dogwood is beautiful in the spring) divides the house from the street above. Dawn fog has settled over the stepping stones and mulch, the light leaking into the sky. Trees appear out of the darkness, ghosts out of milk.

We are leaning on the heavy wood of an enormous turntable, an armoire of a record player. She is whispering to me and the sun is slowly rising. Pale blue carpet and stale cigarette smoke mirror the fog, obscuring faded plaid sofas hulking in corners behind us.

He doesn't want me around our family, she says to me. Her eyes show she is scared and sad, misting. I don't know what to do.

I can talk to him, I say, looking at the blue carpet, the end table, the brass lamps, the vase with the crack.

There's something in the yard, my sister says, suddenly very still. Looking, peering, sensing this from that, attuned to movement.

There it is, I say, and focus into the dawn, damp branches. There is something in the trees, moving in the trees, outside the window. My heartbeat increases, tempted to hold my breath.

Be still and let the movement come, I think to myself. Be still and let it come, it will come and there it is, between the trees.

What is it, she whispers, clutching her small hands between her breasts. What do we do?

Hardly listening, noticing how I have hardly been listening to her as as the form fixes in the windowpanes. Extending my sight toward it, feeling for it, the sky is growing lighter as the sun rises and if I can just touch it, just feel to it. Sense for just a moment

It is rooting in the leaves, looking for food. Hunched, I start to see the shape of it. Arms, long fingers, nibbling branches, tender buds. Head turns, and it is looking at me, the eyes are looking at me and seeing my face, I am seeing the shape of its face and it is a monkey. A two colored monkey, a dark and light monkey with wide eyes and a red collar.

Watching me watch, the monkey slowly abandons the leaves, creeping closer, curious. Looking at my face, head cocked, side steps. Poised and beautiful. There is a thin lead, silver and red, disappearing into the dawn fog.

Let's go, I say to my sister, even as she is tugging on my sleeve. I see the monkey clearly now, and several behind it, and the man with the music box. My sister does not follow me willingly.

Come on, I toss over my shoulder, already throwing the deadbolt on the front door. The smell of morning rushes in with the mist, and rays of grapefruit and orange light are creeping through the blackened branches.

I run through the dawn mist yard into the silent street. The pavement is oddly warm under my feet. In the circle of the cul de sac there are dozens of forms in the mist. I am alone in the street and the streetlight clicks off as the sun rises, a wet breath of shuffling silence. A low whistle passes around the circle.

And then, the day explodes into light and sound. Fireworks rocket and cannons boom and great glittering sequin banners unfurl into absurdity, mylar balloons bursting with stars and stripes and silver chrome. Outrageous arms wave in the air, wigs and animals and instruments. Confetti, and three hundred people scream all at once: happy fourth of july, everybody!

The music commences and I am rushed by monkeys. Suddenly bodies are everywhere, doing all sorts of bodily things. I see there are three monkeys, they are dancing and looking at me, we are being watched by the red music box man.

I look around me, turning in a full circle, the pavement grit. It feels like it does just after sunset, after a long hot afternoon in the sun. Pussywillows grow at the end of the street, and cattails. As the performers whiz by, I see how their eyes flick at me, to see how I am responding. I nod, take a breath.

It's a circus, I say. It must be the fourth of july, and a circus has come to town.

The music is tremendous. It wells and fills the streets, rolling with abandon. All around the neighborhood, I see lights coming on in bedroom windows, sleeping houses roused.

A circus, okay, I say, smiling. I love the circus!

A cheer goes up from the performers. Garlands of flowers heap into the street, horns are blown. Bears on unicycles, mimes juggling bowling pins, stilts and wheels and top hats and cotton candy. Strange gendered creatures of delicate elegance, hybrid creations of ecstatic stature. Velvet nobility, light-bulb lassoes of color. The circus has come to town.

I start to feel the music. I am walking, I am navigating this feast, moving toward the house. I look to the door and my father is there, rushing and running, he is pulling on his pants and shirt and we meet on the sidewalk.

Its okay, I'm saying, it's the just the fourth of july. The circus has come to town, I say, and gesture to the hundreds, the thousands of shiny silver balloons. Shaped like stars, with red and white stripes on them. He is tucking in his shirt and surveying the crowd.

Well, okay, he says. A fat clown on a tiny bicycle rides by, honking a brass horn with a rubber bulb at us. My father's surprise gives way to a look, that look that he gives me that says I disapprove of this. He turns and goes back into the house.

Then it is me and the circus people. The music is good, pleasurable. Rock and roll calliope. Confetti. It is the exact right combination of mayhem and elegance. I am walking through the crowd and looking and looking, and seeing and seeing, what is being changed in hands.

These strangers looking at me, they are looking at my face. I am offered something, taking it in my hand, glancing and noticing the door of the house growing closer and opening. The young man I've been talking to sees the door opening and wants to know if I'm in, if I'd like to participate.

I nod and smile and walk away from the house, not yet ready to return. The crowd presses closer, and a petite woman, a dancer, is standing close to me. Her hair smells delicious. She is wearing street clothes, no costume, casual.

Come dance with me, she says.

She is gorgeous, yearning. Her eyes are dark and her hair hangs softly in ribbons around her face.

Please, come dance, she says, low lilting. The crowd blends, indistinct buzzing. She snakes her arms around my waist and presses close, hips and breast, diminutive and easy in the hollow of my arm. For a moment I feel powerful lusty, she is asking so sweetly, and then someone is standing on the front porch, looking directly at me.

I'll come back, I say, winding my way toward the house. She stands still, watching me go, and a woman is standing on the porch in a blue cardigan sweater and barrettes, worrying her hands. The door is standing open, she is fretting.

Your father is awake, she says. Who was that, were you going to go with her?

Don't worry, it's not like I'm going to run off to the circus, I say.

Walking into the foyer, I shut the door, and the doorbell immediately rings. Not thinking, I turn around and open the door and it's the young man from before, a ringmaster and his friends, and I invite them in for refreshments. They are clumsy around the artifacts, and nearly knock a heavy glass fish paperweight from a curio table.

They sit in the family room, the casual room with the television and brick fireplace, wooden panels and salmon carpet. They settle into the couches and take out pipes. One asks me if we have any understanding or influence over the city noise ordinance. No, I say, and the neighbors are going to be pissed.

I hear my father coming then, and gesture to them to hide their belongings, but they are too slow to catch on. My father stands defiant in the kitchen.

What are they doing here? he says. Hands in loose fists, standing at full height. I say nothing, feeling blush rising in my cheeks, reddening.

What's going on here? he bellows. What are you doing? You're holding their pipe for them, is that it? He points an accusing finger, and I wonder.

Is that what I'm doing?

No, sir. I say, and wave the young men away, out of the room. It was a beautiful circus, I think, waving. The music was wonderful, I remember waking up

And then,

Falling asleep, the face of a genderless desert shadow, crouching on the edge of a canyon in moonlight. Turns and sees me, surprised, and then

I am waking up in a dentist's chair. It's the dentist who looks like a rabbit, the one who once said to me, It's okay. I know what the women like. They all want the *bling*, he says, pointing to his teeth. He knows I am floating on gas he gave me, he is smiling at me, grinning big. White teeth.

He is filing my teeth, my bottom teeth, filing and scraping, putting elbow into it. Can't move, restraints. On the backside of the bottom front teeth, an old filling comes loose, opening a hole.

That's enough for tonight, he says, leaving off. There is the burnt fingernail smell worming in my nose, dentist dust twisting up into sinus cavities. He is long gone by the time the restraints are loosened.

Getting up out of the chair, wandering bare feet and cotton shift into the hallway. Fingers clutching the dislodged piece of tooth, feeling hole gaping in mouth, squirming tongue, twisting tip.

Soft slap of feet padding down the hallway, cold floor. Attendants looking leery through dim fluorescent arches, weird buzzing, watching, trying to smile. It pretends to be a house, a home, an institution. Here is the dentist's bedroom door, and a big sign says NO ONE MAY KNOCK BETWEEN THE HOURS OF. Is it between those hours, I think, knuckles rapping.

What is it, the door opens nervously, what do you need? Showing the piece, the tooth, the stop-gap bloody in the palm of the hand.

We'll take care of that in the morning, he says, taking the tooth from me, shutting the door. Holding that image before me so I can remember, blood on white tooth. Seeing flashes in memory of faces weeping, glistening chins. Muzzled mumbling.

Somehow standing in the kitchen again, clinical. Linoleum and plastic flowers, faded curtains, white light. Standing here staring at kittens, pups, strange little beasts rolling and tumbling on the floor. Somehow the tray of macaroni and cheese is knocked off the counter and they are scarfing it up, they are gorging, even some of the smaller pups are being eaten. I apologize for some reason.

Click teeth and whining. An obnoxious yellow mess of feces and cheese and blood and small animals. One of them has consumed unto death, eaten so much so fast it is choked and unable to breathe. Skin stretched, taut stomach bulging. It vomits as it dies, a paste of food and undeveloped beasts.

Picking it up then, massaging it gently, continuing to disgorge, encouraging passage. It coughs and it breathes again, opening eyes, blinking. Seeing bright blue eyes, clear and clean, recognizing. Feeling stirrings of heart, holding in hands, nurturing palms.

Beginning to see how it all came to this, pregnant, remembering what came before now. When there were huge multicolored rats in circles of light, dim colored ratlights of great violence. Much blood. Realizing the reason for being here in this institution, the plan to take it away, whatever it is that's being carried.

Standing in that broken kitchen and remembering in-between, the night (she) we came here. There was an older man, tanned and wise, gray; this woman remembers him as a medicine man.

He and she and me, we are all coming down the mountain together, where we had gone to help her. We hurry down the road together in the dark, afraid of being caught. Helping him help her, urging us down the mountain and away.

As we walk she sees a dark house on the side of the road, distracting, drawing her. Recognizing it and being trained to go there, thinking we are supposed to go there, be a good girl and go there. There is no time. Dread wells in my chest as she slows, stops.

Wind rustles through dark leaves, creaky porch and wooden windows, blue black boards. Pine trees maybe. This is where he took us sometimes, I think. Flashes of memory try to come, blood and bindings, and I stop them. The gray man turns and looks behind us and recognizes who kept court there, where we took her from. He says the name low to himself and his voice is edged with horror.

He hurries ahead, eager to wave down the lights of a vehicle, get us on board and away before we are noticed. But distance between us grows too quickly in his haste.

I slow down, to make sure she is still with us, that she does not set foot on that looming porch. He is getting further ahead and I am speaking very calmly, very gently. I know it is dangerous to touch her.

Speaking soft and looking at her face, trying to keep her eyes, trying to hold her attention. She stretches to see around me, to see the windows, the steps of the porch. Glancing between her face, the windows, and the headlights behind me, we are somehow getting further away, or at least not closer.

Do not panic. Too far away. Do not panic. Breathing, speaking softly. Urging without urgency, feeling feet on pavement, rising wind. We are too far away. Trees rustling on the dark road, rushes, yawning porch. Bare skin, grit and blacktop firmly underfoot.

Too far, we are too far away. I reach out and touch her, take the hollow of her arm.

She spins to face me as I turn back, we are much further along than estimated, and I make for the road. Seeing my intention, she turns back toward the house with equal force.

I think, If he doesn't get to us in time we'll both be lost. Why was I so distracted, all that fear. Focus, I think, this must be all my fault, focus. Of course he'll come, I say, surely he has flagged help and is returning even now

The immense polarization causes us to spin, she is pulling and we are spinning. Barefoot pirouette, asphalt grinding balls of feet. Holding still as best I can, letting her turn, letting us spin. Redirect trajectory, ballerina musicbox.

Darkness is drawn to our motion. Turning, spiraling, fingers of night filter vision, blackout caressing. Spotting, to keep from getting dizzy. Afterimages, streaks on backs of eyelids, no longer seeing anything at all. Feeling only the gravity of her intention and the waning strength of my resolve, milky enveloping.

Turning on toes, calling out then, into the dark. Open-throated siren song, making a beacon of my voice: you can find me, find me here.

Response or echo comes to my call, can no longer distinguish the difference. Holding on to her. Willing my voice to be heard and hanging on to her, even as we become the darkness

WORKS CITED

1   Śāntideva. *The Bodhicaryavatara: A Guide to the Buddhist Path of Awakening*. Translated by Kate Crosby and Andrew Skilton. Birmingham: Windhorse Publications, 2002. Print.

2   Chernin, Kim. *Reinventing Eve: Modern Woman in Search of Herself.* New York: Harper Perennial, 1987. Print.

3   Gilligan, Carol. *The Birth of Pleasure: A New Map of Love*. New York: Vintage Books, 2003. Print.

4   Campbell, June. *Traveler in Space: In Search of Female Identity in Tibetan Buddhism*. London: Athelone Press, 1996. Print.

5   Brock, Betty. *No Flying in the House*. New York: Scholastic Book Services (a division of Harper and Row), 1970. Print.

6   *Op. cit.* Śāntideva.

7   Newman, John. Translated, *The Heart of the Venerable Mother Prajnaparamita: The Perfection of Wisdom*. Unpublished.

8   Estes, Clarissa Pinkola. *Women Who Run With the Wolves: Myths and Stories of the Wild Woman Archetype*. New York: Ballantine Books, 1992. Print.

9   English, Elizabeth. *Vajrayogini: Her Visualizations, Rituals, and Forms*. Boston: Wisdom Publications, 2002. Print.

10   Wangyal, Tenzin. *The Tibetan Yogas of Dream and Sleep*. Ithaca: Snow Lion, 1998. Print.

11   Godwin, Joscelyn, translator, Adam McClean, commentary. *The Chemical Wedding of Christian Rosenkreutz*. Boston: Phanes Press, 1991. Print.

12   Bachelard, Gaston. *The Poetics of Space*. 1958. Boston: Beacon Press, 1994. Print.

13   Oyama, Susan. "The Problem of Change," *Brain Development and Cognition: A Reader*, ed. Mark H. Johnson. United States: Wiley-Blackwell, 2002. Print.

13-1   Epp, Ellie. "Fields and Networks: An Emerging Archetype," *web. goddard.edu/embodiment/workshops/fields.html.* Web.

14   Rich, Adrienne. *Of Woman Born: Motherhood as Experience and Institution.* New York: W.W. Norton & Company, 1986. Print.

15 & 16   Gross, Rita M. *Buddhism After Patriarchy.* Albany: State University of New York Press, 1993. Print.

17   Gross, Rita M. *A Garland of Feminist Reflections: Forty Years of Religious Exploration.* Berkeley: University of California Press, 2009. Print.

18   Simmer-Brown, Judith. *Dakini's Warm Breath: The Feminine Principle in Tibetan Buddhism.* Boston: Shambhala Publications, 2001. Print.

19   Mor, Barbara. "Hypatia," *Trivia, Voices of Feminism*, issue 7/8, September 2008. http://triviavoices.net/archives/issue7-8/mor.html. Web.

20   Griffin, Susan. *Woman and Nature: The Roaring Inside Her.* San Francisco: Sierra Club Books, 1978. Print.

21   Trungpa, Chogyam. *The Essential Chogyam Trungpa*, edited by Carolyn Rose Gimian. Boston: Shambhala, 1999. Print.

22   Lao-tsu, *Tao Te Ching.* Translated by Gia-fu Feng and Jane English. New York: Vintage Books, 1989. Print.

23   *Op. cit.* Godwin, 1991.

24   *Op cit.* Newman, unpublished.

25   Gray, David B. *The Cakrasamvara Tantra (The Discourse of Sri Heruka), a Study and Annotated Translation.* New York: American Institute of Buddhist Studies at Columbia University, 2007. Print.

26   Maso, Carole. *Break Every Rule: Essays on Language, Longing, & Moments of Desire*. Washington D.C.: Counterpoint, 2000. Print.

27   *Op. cit.* Chernin, 1987.

28   Blakeslee, Sandra and Matthew Blakeslee. *The Body Has a Mind of Its Own: How Body Maps in Your Brain Help You Do Almost (Everything) Better*. New York: Random House, 2007. Print.

29   Anderson, Rosemarie. "Embodied Writing and Reflections on Embodiment," *Journal of Transpersonal Psychology*, vol. 33-2, p. 83-98: 2001. integral-inquiry.com/cybrary/embodied.htm. Web.

30   Gyatso, Tenzin, H.H. XIV Dalai Lama, and Tsongkhapa. Trans. & ed. Jeffery Hopkins. *Yoga Tantra: Paths to Magical Feats*. Ithaca: Snow Lion Publications, 2005. Print.

31   White, David Gordon, ed. *Tantra In Practice*. Princeton: Princeton University Press, 2000. Print.

32   Cohen, Leonard. *Stranger Music*. New York: Vintage Books: 1993. Print.

33   Crowley, Aleister. *Liber AL vel Legis*. San Francisco: Weiser Books, 2004. Print.

34   Lakoff, George and Mark Johnson. *Philosophy in the Flesh: The Embodied Mind and its Challenge to Western Thought*. New York: Basic Books, 1999. Print.

35   *Op. cit.* Rich, 1986.

36   Ray, Reginald. *Touching Enlightenment: Finding Realization in the Body*. Boulder: Sounds True Inc., 2008. Print.

37   Chalmers, David J. *Philosophy of Mind: Classical and Contemporary Readings*. Oxford: Oxford University Press, 2002. Print.

38   Wallace, B. Alan. *The Taboo of Subjectivity: Toward a New Science of Consciousness.* New York: Oxford University Press, 2000. Print.

39   Blackmore, Susan. *Consciousness: An Introduction.* New York: Oxford University Press, 2004. Print.

www.ingramcontent.com/pod-product-compliance
Lightning Source LLC
Chambersburg PA
CBHW020932090426
42736CB00010B/1110